1,000,000 Books

are available to read at

Forgotten Books

www.ForgottenBooks.com

Read online
Download PDF
Purchase in print

ISBN 978-1-330-12195-5
PIBN 10031083

This book is a reproduction of an important historical work. Forgotten Books uses state-of-the-art technology to digitally reconstruct the work, preserving the original format whilst repairing imperfections present in the aged copy. In rare cases, an imperfection in the original, such as a blemish or missing page, may be replicated in our edition. We do, however, repair the vast majority of imperfections successfully; any imperfections that remain are intentionally left to preserve the state of such historical works.

Forgotten Books is a registered trademark of FB &c Ltd.
Copyright © 2018 FB &c Ltd.
FB &c Ltd, Dalton House, 60 Windsor Avenue, London, SW19 2RR.
Company number 08720141. Registered in England and Wales.

For support please visit www.forgottenbooks.com

1 MONTH OF FREE READING

at

www.ForgottenBooks.com

By purchasing this book you are eligible for one month membership to ForgottenBooks.com, giving you unlimited access to our entire collection of over 1,000,000 titles via our web site and mobile apps.

To claim your free month visit: www.forgottenbooks.com/free31083

* Offer is valid for 45 days from date of purchase. Terms and conditions apply.

English
Français
Deutsche
Italiano
Español
Português

www.forgottenbooks.com

Mythology Photography **Fiction**
Fishing Christianity **Art** Cooking
Essays Buddhism Freemasonry
Medicine **Biology** Music **Ancient Egypt** Evolution Carpentry Physics
Dance Geology **Mathematics** Fitness
Shakespeare **Folklore** Yoga Marketing
Confidence Immortality Biographies
Poetry **Psychology** Witchcraft
Electronics Chemistry History **Law**
Accounting **Philosophy** Anthropology
Alchemy Drama Quantum Mechanics
Atheism Sexual Health **Ancient History**
Entrepreneurship Languages Sport
Paleontology Needlework Islam
Metaphysics Investment Archaeology
Parenting Statistics Criminology
Motivational

SCHOOL COSTS AND SCHOOL ACCOUNTING

BY

J. HOWARD HUTCHINSON

SUBMITTED IN PARTIAL FULFILLMENT OF THE REQUIREMENTS
FOR THE DEGREE OF DOCTOR OF PHILOSOPHY
IN THE FACULTY OF PHILOSOPHY,
COLUMBIA UNIVERSITY

PUBLISHED BY
Teachers College, Columbia University
NEW YORK CITY
1913

COPYRIGHT, 1914, BY J. HOWARD HUTCHINSON

PREFACE

Whatever value is possessed by this dissertation comes from the kindness and courtesy of the superintendents of schools and from school accounting officers who so willingly made available the data in their possession concerning the cost of education in their school systems and the methods employed in accounting for school funds. Their number alone prevents acknowledgment being made to them individually. To them also must acknowledgment be made for permission to use copies of forms and records for purposes of illustration. To Professor George D. Strayer of Teachers College, Columbia University, the author is particularly obligated for guidance while making the investigation and for wise suggestions and criticism in the treatment of the data collected. The opportunities afforded by a year with the Training School for Public Service of the Bureau of Municipal Research, New York City, increased the worth of the constructive aspect of the study. Finally, to my wife should acknowledgment be made for aid in the detailed study of the data and for inspiration and suggestion in their treatment.

CONTENTS

Chapter		Page
I.	Introduction	1

PART I. A STUDY OF SCHOOL COSTS

II.	Purposes of School Accounting	4
III.	Purpose of This Investigation	10
IV.	Annual Financial Statements of Some Boards of Education	12
V.	Amounts Spent by Twenty Cities for the Education of Each Pupil in Average Daily Attendance	20
VI.	Problem One: Cost per Pupil in Average Daily Attendance on All Schools	32
VII.	Problem Two: Cost per Pupil in Average Daily Attendance on Each Kind of School	37
VIII.	Problem Three: Cost per Pupil in Average Daily Attendance for Each Character of Service	47
IX.	Problem Four: Cost per Pupil in Average Daily Attendance for Personal Service, Supplies, and Various Services	53

PART II. A STUDY OF SCHOOL ACCOUNTING

X.	Description and Use of Documents of Expenditure	56

    A. Requisitions.
    B. Purchase Orders.
    C. Payrolls.
    D. Vouchers.

XI.	Description and Use of Various Ledgers	77
XII.	Description and Use of Financial Statements	86

PART III. A SYSTEM OF SCHOOL ACCOUNTING RECOMMENDED

                                                            PAGE

XIII. PURPOSES TO BE SERVED BY THE ACCOUNTING SYSTEM RECOMMENDED 98

XIV. DESCRIPTION AND USE OF EXPENDITURE DOCUMENTS RECOMMENDED... 101
- A. Requisitions.
- B. Purchase Orders.
- C. Vouchers.
- D. Payrolls.

XV. DESCRIPTION AND USE OF VARIOUS LEDGERS RECOMMENDED. 122
- A. Expense Ledger.
- B. Property Ledger.
- C. Supply and Text-book Ledger.
- D. Supply and Text-book Tag.
- E. Appropriation Ledger.

XVI. DESCRIPTION AND USE OF FINANCIAL STATEMENTS......... 131
- A. General Balance Sheet.
- B. Statement of Expenditures.
- C. Monthly Property Statement.
- D. Distribution of Expense Sheet.
- E. Statement of Unit Costs.

XVII. CONCLUSION.. 146

INDEX.. 147

LIST OF TABLES

			PAGE
TABLE	I.	LIST OF CITIES VISITED AND THEIR POPULATIONS..	2
TABLE	II.	STATEMENT OF ITEMS FOR WHICH UNIT COSTS WERE SOUGHT	11
TABLE	III.	STATEMENT OF EXPENDITURES OF CITY F	12
TABLE	IV.	STATEMENT OF EXPENDITURES OF CITY L	13
TABLE	V.	STATEMENT OF EXPENDITURES OF CITY M	13
TABLE	VI.	STATEMENT OF EXPENDITURES OF CITY V	14
TABLE	VII.	STATEMENT OF EXPENDITURES OF CITY T	14
TABLE	VIII.	STATEMENT OF EXPENDITURES OF CITY C	15
TABLE	IX.	STATEMENT OF EXPENDITURES OF CITY A	16
TABLE	X.	STATEMENT OF EXPENDITURES OF CITY E	17
TABLE	XI.	STATEMENT OF EXPENDITURES OF CITY W	18, 19
TABLE	XII.	AVERAGE DAILY ATTENDANCE ON ALL SCHOOLS, ELEMENTARY SCHOOLS, AND HIGH SCHOOLS, IN TWENTY CITIES	20
TABLE	XIII.	AMOUNTS SPENT PER PUPIL IN AVERAGE DAILY ATTENDANCE ON THE SCHOOLS OF TWENTY CITIES	22–31
TABLE	XIV.	TOTAL EXPENDITURES PER PUPIL IN AVERAGE DAILY ATTENDANCE ON ALL SCHOOLS	32
TABLE	XV.	AMOUNTS SPENT FOR EACH KIND OF SCHOOL AS SHOWN IN THE STATEMENT FROM CITY C	37
TABLE	XVI.	AMOUNTS SPENT FOR EACH KIND OF SCHOOL AS SHOWN IN THE STATEMENT FROM CITY W	42
TABLE	XVII.	AMOUNTS SPENT FOR EACH KIND OF SCHOOL AS SHOWN IN THE STATEMENT FROM CITY G	45
TABLE	XVIII.	AMOUNTS SPENT FOR EACH KIND OF SCHOOL AS SHOWN IN THE STATEMENT FROM CITY H	46
TABLE	XIX.	AMOUNTS SPENT FOR OPERATION AS GIVEN IN THE STATEMENTS FROM SIX CITIES	51
TABLE	XX.	EXPENDITURE PER PUPIL IN AVERAGE DAILY ATTENDANCE FOR OPERATION OF SCHOOLS IN SIX CITIES	51
TABLE	XXI.	AMOUNTS SPENT PER PUPIL IN AVERAGE DAILY ATTENDANCE FOR PERSONAL SERVICE FOR EDUCATION IN EIGHT CITIES	54
TABLE	XXII.	SUMMARY OF THE DATA CONTAINED AND REQUIRED ON THE REQUISITION FORMS IN USE IN SIXTEEN CITIES	58–60
TABLE	XXIII.	SUMMARY OF THE DATA CONTAINED AND REQUIRED ON THE ORDER FORMS IN USE IN ELEVEN CITIES	65, 66
TABLE	XXIV.	SUMMARY OF THE DATA CONTAINED AND REQUIRED ON THE PAYROLLS IN USE IN EIGHTEEN CITIES	70–72
TABLE	XXV.	SUMMARY OF THE DATA CONTAINED AND REQUIRED ON THE VOUCHERS IN USE IN TEN CITIES	75, 76

LIST OF FORMS RECOMMENDED

	PAGE
REQUISITION FOR TEXT-BOOKS AND SUPPLIES	102
WORK REQUISITION	106
PURCHASE ORDER	110
PAYMENT VOUCHER	114
ELEMENTARY SCHOOL PAYROLL	116
ELEMENTARY SCHOOL PRINCIPAL'S TIME SHEET	116
SUPERVISORS' AND SPECIAL TEACHERS' PAYROLL	118
SUPERVISORS' AND SPECIAL TEACHERS' TIME SHEET	118
GRADE LEDGER SHEET	123
GENERAL ADMINISTRATION SHEET	123
SCHOOL LEDGER SHEET	124
PROPERTY LEDGER SHEET	124
SUPPLY AND TEXT-BOOK RECORD SHEET	128
SUPPLY AND TEXT-BOOK TAG	129
APPROPRIATION LEDGER	130
MONTHLY BALANCE SHEET	132
MONTHLY STATEMENT OF EXPENDITURES	134
MONTHLY PROPERTY STATEMENT	134
STATEMENT OF SUPPLIES AND TEXT-BOOKS IN USE	136
EXPENSE DISTRIBUTION SHEET	140–141
MONTHLY STATEMENT OF UNIT COSTS	144–145

SCHOOL COSTS AND SCHOOL ACCOUNTING

CHAPTER I

INTRODUCTION

The purpose of this investigation was to determine standard unit costs of public education.

Thirty-eight cities were visited in order to obtain the data necessary. Superintendents were asked for a statement of the expense of running their schools during the last financial year. They gave what data they could in one of two ways: (1) by referring the writer to the books, from which he obtained such information as they had to offer, and (2) by referring the writer to the last annual report, which he used only after the superintendent had said that it was a true statement of the expenditures for carrying on the activities of the school board for the year named. The latter data were used only when the books of record were unavailable.

Two other inquiries were made to learn: (1) the original documents used in recording transactions and the facts contained in such documents, and (2) the final disposition made of the data contained in the original documents. That is, information was obtained concerning the forms and books used in recording expenditures and accounting for funds.

During the first part of the investigation the information concerning forms and records was considered merely as incidental, as possibly interesting in some supplementary study. But as the investigation proceeded, the character of the cost data collected made apparent the importance of studying the records kept of school expenditures.

Naturally it was desired to make the investigation productive of results that would be useful to the greatest number of school officials. To do this it was necessary that cities be chosen for study that were typical of American cities in general and so did not vary too much in size of population. Therefore the limits set were 10,000 and 100,000, for between these limits are found by far the greatest number of cities.

In Table I is given the list of cities visited and the population of each.

TABLE I
Cities Visited and Their Populations

Name of City	Population
Little Falls, N. Y.*	12,273
Geneva, N. Y.*	12,446
Port Chester, N. Y.*	12,809
Framingham, Mass.	12,948
Marlborough, Mass.	14,579
Bloomfield, N. J.*	15,070
Melrose, Mass.*	15,715
Lockport, N. Y.*	17,970
Revere, Mass.	18,219
Beverly, Mass.	18,650
Northampton, Mass.	19,431
Montclair, N. J.*	21,550
New Brunswick, N. J.*	23,388
Brookline, Mass.	27,792
Newburgh, N. Y.*	27,805
Poughkeepsie, N. Y.*	27,936
Stamford, Conn.*	28,836
New Rochelle, N. Y.	28,867
Orange, N. J.	29,630
Niagara Falls, N. Y.*	30,445
Mount Vernon, N. Y.*	30,919
Amsterdam, N. Y.*	31,267
Chelsea, Mass.	32,452
Everett, Mass.*	33,484
East Orange, N. J.	34,371
Auburn, N. Y.	34,668
Elmira, N. Y.	37,176
Newton, Mass.	39,806
Malden, Mass.*	44,404
Binghamton, N. Y.*	48,443
Passaic, N. J.	54,773
Bayonne, N. J.	55,545
Hoboken, N. J.	70,324
Schenectady, N. Y.	72,826
Utica, N. Y.*	74,419
Somerville, Mass.	77,236
Yonkers, N. Y.*	79,803
Lynn, Mass.*	89,336

Introduction

The star placed after the names of certain of the cities listed indicates that the data of expenditures obtained from them are used in the treatment of costs that follows. Financial data from the other cities were not made use of for one or more of these reasons: (1) because the data available were so incomplete as to make them useless; (2) because different methods of distribution of expenditures were employed by different cities, with no indication of the methods used or of the warrants for their use, which introduced a factor causing variability that should not be allowed to influence the results; (3) because the data could not be found in the superintendent's office by those in charge of them; (4) because of the unwillingness of the person in charge to permit examination of the books—in one case because of the absence of the superintendent; in the other case because the superintendent had no authority over such officer to dispel his unwillingness.

The results of the investigation are presented under the three following headings:

1. A Study of School Costs.
2. A Study of School Accounting.
3. A System of School Accounting Recommended.

PART I. A STUDY OF SCHOOL COSTS

CHAPTER II

PURPOSES OF SCHOOL ACCOUNTING

Of all the subjects presented at the 1913 meeting of the *Department of Superintendence* of the National Education Association, none was so productive of discussion as that of standardization in school work. Time and again was the subject touched upon directly or indirectly by its advocates; and more often did speakers mention it so as to bring a laugh at the expense of those who would standardize all that is possible of standardization in education. The magic word efficiency that is causing such a revolution in industry is beginning to work in education. As in industry, so in education, efficiency is based on complete knowledge. That administrative officers have not yet demanded and obtained knowledge sufficient to enable their school systems to work at anything like high efficiency is shown by statements made at this meeting; and the fact that the statements were made shows that there is felt a need for more knowledge.

Two men, one United States Commissioner of Education, the other Auditor of the Board of Education of New York City, are reported to have repeated the statement that figures or statistics may "make or unmake policies." It is from quantitative data that the best and only truly accurate measure of methods can be obtained. Before standardization can take place data must be provided; and before data can be provided there must have been installed the mechanism for their collection. Our purpose is to standardize school costs. The accomplishment of the purpose depends upon the data collected and these in turn upon the mechanism provided for their collection.

One of the speakers at the meeting of the National Education Association stated again the oft-repeated but nearly worn-out excuse for educational inefficiency when he said that the amount of money appropriated for education determines the amount of education provided. The statement is true and is not true. A critic of present-day educational administration is perfectly right in saying that the statement is not true. At any rate, we do know that no more does the city that spends most for education turn out the most efficient citizens than does the city that spends least for education turn out the least efficient citizens. The city that spends more than is necessary does as much harm through the benefits that are lacking because of wasted funds, as the city that spends less than is necessary does through the benefits that are lacking because of inadequate funds.

The amount of money spent by municipalities for education is increasing much more rapidly than the population. The financial requirements of education are to-day greater than those of any other service performed by the community. It has often been said that the limit to the money that can be spent for educational purposes will soon be reached. Certain communities have already reached their limit. In these cities the individuals in control—they may be members of school boards or persons working through members of school boards—decide upon the maximum tax rate that their city can levy without driving industries away or keeping them from coming to their community, and fix the allowance for education accordingly. Expenditures for training children cannot continue to increase in the future as they have increased in the past. But the qualifications required of the individual are continually becoming higher, more general, and more specialized. These make necessary more and better training. That is, for the same expenditure of money there must be an increasing return in education. That is, again, the percentage of efficiency of a school system, instead of being from 15 per cent to 35 per cent, as it now is stated to be, must approach 100 per cent.

By this time the query has probably occurred: How will the determination of standard unit costs for education increase school efficiency?

Again to refer to the discussions of the superintendents attending the National Education Association, it is refreshing to find a school man emphasizing that which, though common to school work and industry, is not emphasized in school work as it is in industry where it has been found to be indispensable. Superintendent Spaulding of Newton, Mass., read a paper upon "Applied Scientific Management," in which he showed how a knowledge of the cost per pupil of instruction in each subject in the high schools of Newton helped to determine the action of the authorities with regard to future instruction in those subjects. He drove his point home by emphasizing the preposterousness of delegating to one officer full charge of the financial side of a school system and to another coördinate officer full charge of the educational side of a school system. Would a shoe manufacturing concern, he asked, give to one official full control over the finances, the determination of the expenditures of the concern, and to another full charge of the manufacturing of shoes, paying no attention to the cost of such production? The answer is obvious. Producing shoes without regard to costs is the first step in bankruptcy proceedings. Some time administration of education without regard to costs will be sufficient evidence of inefficiency of administrative officers.

Accounting serves three purposes: (1) From it can be learned whether those persons to whom funds have been entrusted have used those funds as they report they used them. (2) By it can be determined policies in regard to the work of an organization as a whole or in any of its parts. (3) Through it those in authority may discover the efficiency of persons employed and methods and equipment used.

The first purpose is served in a school system when the items and amounts of appropriations are listed, when evidence of expenditures is recorded together with the evidence of proper receipt of goods and services, when such expenditures are charged against the proper items of appropriation, when it can at any time be shown what is the recorded balance on hand of any appropriation and when there is the evidence that such balance is on hand. The purpose of such accounting is to insure the fidelity of the individuals entrusted with the funds. The following is a good example of such accounting as it is required of the Board of Education of City X.

CITY X

1910

FINANCIAL EXHIBIT

TUITION

Appropriation...................	$107,500.00		
Receipts......................	43.50		
Transfer from contingent.........		$ 1,836.60	
			$109,380.10
By pay rolls....................		109,380.10	

SALARIES

Appropriation...................	$ 18,500.00		
Receipts......................	24.00		
Transfer from contingent.........	69.43		
		$18,593.43	
By salaries paid................			$ 18,593.43

INCIDENTALS AND SUPPLIES

Appropriation...................	$ 12,500.00		
Receipts......................	268.49		
		$12,768.49	
By bills paid...................		11,752.89	
Balance to contingent...........			$1,015.60

SCHOOL BLDGS., CARE AND REPAIR

Appropriation...................	$ 6,000.00		
Receipts......................	121.30		
Transfer from contingent.........	590.00		
		$ 6,711.30	
By bills paid...................		6,325.88	
Balance to contingent...........			$385.42

FUEL

Appropriation...................	$7,700.00	$7,700.00	
By bills paid...................		7,049.08	
Balance to contingent...........			$650.92

This board of education, through its employees, kept account of each fund and charged against the proper fund each expenditure, but only after the receipt of goods or services had been certified to by an employee and the expenditure had been endorsed by a committee of the board. At the end of the year this board presented its report as above, which is in brief, "At the beginning of the fiscal year we received the amounts indicated, to be expended for the purposes and things named. Expenditures have been made to the amounts stated, vouchers for the same being filed in the office of the secretary. The balances as stated are on hand, of which the records and names of depositories may be seen upon application to the secretary." And following the original statement is probably an affidavit to the same effect, signed by the president as representing the board of education.

An inquisitive citizen could, from the accounting kept by this board of education, learn whether or not it was faithful to the trust imposed in it, i.e., whether it spent the money as it stated it did. However, all of these expenditures were really made for the purpose of purchasing the performance of certain services or functions. Suppose an inquisitive citizen, jealous of his wealth, should ask, "How much did we spend for high schools last year?" "How much was that per pupil?" "How does that compare with the cost per pupil a year before?" No information could be given him. Indeed no information at all is given of the amount of service purchased for the expenditures and of the cost per unit of that service.

The second and third purposes of accounting, commonly called cost accounting, are to express expenditures in terms of output, of work done, of services rendered. This phase of accounting is more recent than the former. It is found chiefly in private concerns, having made little headway in municipal accounting. It came as the result of keen competition in the industrial world. The manufacturer was obliged to make a certain profit. To do this he had to sell at a price not above that of his competitors. So to be certain of covering all the expense of manufacture and to insure the profit desired he had to know accurately the costs of production. Again, by accounting for each process in the manufacture of an article, the manufacturer can continually cheapen production by trying new methods of performing certain operations and comparing the costs of these with the methods previously used. But probably the most important use of cost accounting is to measure efficiency. By learning the cost per unit for performing the various steps in the production of an article, by comparing it with previous costs and usual costs, it can be known at once when any changes have taken place in the performance of the work and from that the causes of such changes. When one department or one man is turning out more work, the matter becomes known and can be investigated and perhaps the new method can be used in other departments and by other men to increase their efficiency. The chief usefulness of cost accounting is to measure the efficiency of work done.

From the above can be inferred the importance of determining standard costs of education. What a lawn mower, a stationary engine, or a locomotive should cost is known. It is known what one should spend to construct a house of a certain kind, to keep a hen for a certain period, to raise a spring lamb; but no one knows how much should be spent to educate a child; it is not even known how much should be spent to give a child one year's schooling.

A study of sufficient cities should enable one to determine what ought to be the cost of instructing a child in each kind of school. Such standards would enable cities to determine whether they are doing right by their youth; they would serve as a guide to them. Such standards would enable those interested in education to test the efficiency of the educational performance of any city. That is, standard unit costs for education would serve as tests which, together with other tests, could be used by those within and by those without a school system to determine the efficiency of educational production.

CHAPTER III

PURPOSE OF THIS INVESTIGATION

The original purpose of this study as stated before was to determine *standard unit costs for public education.* It is well at once to define these terms as they are used in this study.

Education is used to include only that instruction and training which is provided in institutions existing for that stated purpose. By *public education* is meant that instruction and training which is obtained through the expenditure of funds voted by citizens of a municipality (together with contributions from other sources) and administered by duly authorized representatives of such citizens.

By the *cost of public education* is meant all the expense incurred in providing instruction and training by means of funds voted by the citizens of a municipality and contributed to the citizens of a municipality for that purpose.

The term *unit costs* for public education is used to mean the total cost of public education as well as the costs of any part of it, divided by the total number of units of any one kind that determine the total cost of public education or any part of it. Thus, some of the kinds of units that determine such costs are schools, school rooms, subjects taught, pupils taught, districts, and city wards. The unit used in this discussion is "pupil in average daily attendance," because it is a physical constant that is easily and accurately ascertainable, having to all persons the same meaning.

The word *standard* contains the idea of authority based upon numbers. Standard units are units that have authority because of the frequency of their occurrence. Unit costs of public education would be standard when such unit costs were practically identical for many cities.

The purpose then in determining standard unit costs of public education is to provide the school administrator with certain tests which, with other tests, especially of pupils' abilities, will enable him to determine the efficiency of his own school system by comparing the costs per pupil in average daily attendance for public education in his own system with the costs in many school systems.

The plural form of the word cost is used because to be worth while the study must reveal the standard unit costs, not only of the one great service public education, but also of the many distinct services that make up public education. That is, to be worth while, this study must determine not only the standard total unit cost for public education, i.e., for all schools, but also the standard unit cost for each kind of public education, i.e., for all elementary schools, for all high schools. Nor is this sufficient. For all schools and for each kind of school there should be determined the standard unit costs for each character of service rendered, i.e., administration, operation, etc. And finally, to be complete, there must be determined for all schools, for each kind of school, and for each character of expenditure for each kind of school and all schools, the standard unit cost of each object of expenditure, as of personal service, of supplies, etc.

The purpose of this study given in detail was the following:

To determine the standard cost for public education for each pupil in average daily attendance for each item in Table II distributed as indicated.

TABLE II

ITEMS FOR WHICH UNIT COSTS WERE SOUGHT FROM THE STUDY OF THE SCHOOL EXPENSES OF TWENTY CITIES

	ALL SCHOOLS	ELEMENTARY SCHOOLS	HIGH SCHOOLS	VOCATIONAL SCHOOLS	EVENING SCHOOLS
TOTAL: Total cost, Personal service, Supplies, Various services					
ADMINISTRATION: Total cost, Personal service, Supplies, Various services					
SUPERVISION: Total cost, Personal service, Supplies, Various services					
INSTRUCTION: Total cost, Personal service, Supplies, Various services					
OPERATION: Total cost, Personal service, Supplies, Various services					
MAINTENANCE: Total cost, Personal service, Supplies, Various services					

CHAPTER IV

ANNUAL FINANCIAL STATEMENTS OF SOME BOARDS OF EDUCATION

In attempting to determine the unit costs of education there were obtained from twenty cities the fullest statements possible of the expenses for education for the last financial year of which records were available. The original forms of the statements were changed as far as necessary in order to have them arranged uniformly so as to facilitate comparison. There are given in Tables III to XI inclusive nine of these statements representing three that are regarded as the poorest, three as ordinary and three that are considered as the best of the twenty examined. The statements given here have been further modified to make them less unwieldy while in no way injuring their usefulness, by omitting the expenditures for certain elementary schools when expenditures as originally reported had been distributed to all schools and the data concerning two or three elementary schools were sufficiently descriptive of all. All data omitted here are on file in the *D*epartment of Educational Administration, Teachers College, Columbia University, New York City, where they may be examined by those desiring to do so.

Tables III to V inclusive contain the three financial statements that are regarded as the poorest; Tables VI to VIII those that are considered fair or ordinary; and Tables IX to XI inclusive those that are considered the best of the twenty examined.

TABLE III

Annual Financial Statement of City F

Teachers' Wages	$55,711.58
High School Teachers	19,515.77
Repairs	17,148.36
Furniture, etc.	1,028.29
Library	682.61
Contingent	15,311.58
Bonds and Interest	7,680.00
Total	$117,078.19

TABLE IV
ANNUAL FINANCIAL STATEMENT OF CITY L

Teachers and Superintendent	$48,225.92
Repairs	780.18
Fuel	4,103.34
Library	534.20
Compulsory Education	400.00
Night School	213.50
Medical Inspection	240.00
Contingent Expenses	6,194.68
Bonds due May 1, 1911	6,000.00
Interest May 1, 1911	720.00
Interest Due November 1, 1911	600.00
Total	$68,011.82

TABLE V
ANNUAL FINANCIAL STATEMENT OF CITY M

Superintendent and Teachers	$66,200.72
Pensions	664.00
Total	$66,864.72
Janitors and Attendance Officers	5,251.09
Clerk	200.00
Census	100.00
Interest on Bonds	7,378.27
Insurance	32.80
New Furniture	1,400.00
Annual Instalment on Bonds	5,067.00
First National Bank	10,800.00
Repair of Buildings	952.22
Fuel	1,720.86
Books	2,326.20
Supplies	2,268.88
Apparatus and Reference Books	136.16
Contingent	
Cartage, Freight and Express	145.61
Tuning Piano	31.00
Laundry	110.34
Printing and Advertising	303.85
Assessment Roll	75.00
Legal Services	155.00
Water Rent	146.32
Gas and Electricity	89.89
Postage	26.96
Telephone	180.41
Bill Posting	16.00
Rent of Hall—Annual Meeting	20.00
Sundry Supplies	1,409.24
Expenses of Superintendent	198.91
Interest on Loan	102.44
Assessment and Taxes	216.54
Washington Park School	20,460.60
Brookville School Addition	10,361.57
Total	$138,547.88
Grand Total	$205,412.60

TABLE VI
Annual Financial Statement of City V

	Total	Grammar Schools	High School	Night School
Board of Education*	$4,890.00			
Superintendent	3,740.69			
Supervisors	11,775.00	$11,775.00		
Principals	22,800.00	17,500.00	$5,300.00	
Teachers	137,832.36	102,018.83	33,108.53	$2,705.00
Text-books	6,114.66	4,500.03	1,614.63	
Stationery, etc.	2,153.72	885.29	1,039.33	229.10
Janitors	13,093.04	11,266.84	1,826.20	
Fuel and Light	9,181.62	7,782.75	1,398.87	
Library	13,370.00	12,033.00	1,337.00	
Teachers' Retirement Fund	4,115.44	3,480.63	634.81	
Water, Janitors' Supplies, etc.	13,886.82	11,891.06	1,995.76	
Repairs and Insurance	10,833.29	8,504.94	2,328.35	
Bonds	7,000.00	7,000.00		
Interest	22,611.50	19,411.50	3,200.00	
Total	$283,398.14	$218,049.87	$53,783.48	$2,934.10

* Includes clerk, stenographer, attendance officer.

TABLE VII
Annual Financial Statement of City T

	Total	High School	School A	School B	School C
School Library	$23.72				
Academy Library					
Public Library	1,100.00				
Free Text-books	5.50				
School Apparatus	111.55	$69.25			$14.00
School Supplies	695.76	35.19			
School Sites (New and Improved)					
School Houses (New and Improved)	520.33	165.00	$109.30	$99.65	
Rent of School Houses					
Repair of School Houses	1,527.42	229.24	176.26	245.83	78.73
Insurance	1,441.10	265.00	120.00	227.50	247.00
Repairs (Fences, Walks, Lawns, etc.)	345.87	19.23			168.54
Printing, Stationery and Postage	1,047.49				
Heat, Light and Power	4,003.38				
Water Taxes	290.86				5.07
Janitors' Tools and Supplies	9.80			1.10	1.50
Care of Truants	2.00				
School Census					
Miscellaneous	1,205.81	22 32			
Salaries of Teachers	52,061.74				
Salaries of other Employees	9,616.00				
Furniture (New and Repaired)	590.82	98.95	53.65	77.77	11.10
Totals	$74,599.15	$904.18	$459.21	$651.85	$525.94

TABLE VIII
ANNUAL FINANCIAL STATEMENT OF CITY C

	TOTAL	HIGH SCHOOL	SCHOOL A	SCHOOL B	SCHOOL C	SCHOOL D
BUILDING FUND						
Sites..............	$44,613.22	$43,013.22				
Repairs............	4,249.65	63.65	$376.25	$86.47	$797.22	$141.32
Improvement of Grounds.........	171.44	45.44	48.17			
Leases.............	125.00	125.00				
TEACHERS' FUND.....	125,679.89	25,526.50	8,258.50	2,882.50	9,739.25	8,262.91
GENERAL FUND						
Fuel..............	755.06	23.83	29.16	7.20	48.94	1.80
Janitors and Labor..	11,686.68	1,711.59	627.66	728.00	1,035.84	634.98
Supplies and Repairs	3,806.23	767.41	168.91	61.64	406.70	207.58
Total..........	$191,087.17	$71,276.64	$9,508.65	$3,765.81	$12,027.95	$9,248.59
Superintendent.......	$3,000.00					
Supervisor of Music...	1,250.00					
Supervisor of Drawing	500.00					
Truant Teacher.......	431.25					
Tuition Orphan Home.	300.00					
Gas and Electricity....	624.06					
Insurance............	916.42					
Board Printing.......	123.00					
High School Printing..	178.56					
Ward School Printing.	144.89					
Secretary's salary.....	1,200.00					
Attendance Officer....	720.00					
Stenographer.........	494.00					
Office and Miscellaneous............	521.58					
LIBRARY AND BOOK FUND						
Pictures............	50.47					
Text-books........	2,470.92					
Apparatus..........	221.49					
NIGHT SCHOOL FUND						
Teachers' Wages....	792.00					
Supplies...........	11.65					
Total..........	$13,950.29					
Grand Total.....	$205,037.46					

TABLE IX

ANNUAL FINANCIAL STATEMENT OF CITY A

	TOTAL	SCHOOL A	SCHOOL B	SCHOOL C	HIGH SCHOOL	ADMINISTRATION
Binding............	$473.04		$1.00		$12.70	$459.34
Clocks.............	199.69		2.00	$2.50	97.51	2.70
Drawing Material....	995.85	$21.14	89.55	66.46	127.13	94.47
Electric Light and Power.............	1,173.76	8.08	19.27	36.21	779.62	
Express............	194.52	2.75	2.45	3.00	45.13	78.60
Flags..............	74.33		2.89	2.89		39.02
Furniture...........	968.23	9.47	8.46	12.97	237.26	320.82
Gas................	78.84			3.08	42.83	5.10
Graduation.........	381.42		6.82	6.52	82.42	219.29
Janitor's Supplies.....	824.13	13.80	3.59	8.05	74.95	528.49
Labor..............	640.50	7.55	17.90	21.91	72.18	378.65
Manual Training.....	877.86		.80		570.04	134.81
Maps and Globes.....	181.41	4.95	1.89	19.60	78.09	1.50
Postage............	10.79	.05	.14	.32	.10	9.32
Printing............	426.34				188.75	237.59
Science............	205.85				205.85	
Sewing.............	81.82	2.04	2.50	21.71		18.67
Blanks.............	313.19	.15	11.51	14.40	105.54	70.22
Busy Work.........	124.90	22.85	.53	2.60		42.77
Erasers............	73.21		4.00	.80	32.09	13.00
Ink................	88.52			8.63	33.77	27.82
Paper..............	1,828.14	21.12	43.39	96.41	799.01	179.69
Pens...............	119.89	4.01	6.55		20.80	12.00
Pencils.............	138.15	3.28	4.15	1.60	15.53	36.61
Sundries...........	341.75	1.48	14.61	3.50	52.51	209.39
Telephone..........	341.75		18.03	13.78	48.72	95.39
Towels and Soap.....	311.16	3.30	7.10	10.78	126.81	4.38
Travel.............	224.65			12.70		128.94
Truants............	328.15					328.15
Typewriters........	387.41				378.06	9.35
Cooking............	199.02					199.02
Total..........	$12,608.27	$126.02	$269.13	$370.42	$4,227.40	$3,885.15
Directors...........	$4,040.71					$4,040.71
Employees and Helpers	2,429.49				$816.50	1,563.40
Janitors............	15,838.03	$598.36	$648.22	$847.67	5,322.29	
Regular Teachers.....	140,491.31	3,297.67	4,534.58	9,272.45	41,021.17	547.71
Substitute Teachers...	4,965.62	167.50	30.00	206.80	612.00	1,378.87
Superintendents and Supervising Principals...............	19,865.53		1,650.00	1,800.00	2,600.00	2,700.00
Truant Officers.......	725.00					725.00
Total..........	$188,355.69	$4,063.53	$6,862.80	$12,126.92	$50,371.96	$10,955.69
Text-books.........	$5,244.13	$93.37	$311.57	$310.21	$964.92	$48.85
Water..............	777.72	10.88	8.32	28.48	282.10	28.48
Medical Inspection...	650.11					650.11
Drinking Fountains...	92.93		56.94		4.51	19.98
Evening Schools.....	5,474.59					3,397.56
Drawing School.....	686.29					686.29
Manual Training Fund	37.17				25.99	4.28
Total..........	$12,962.94	$104.25	$376.83	$338.69	$1,277.52	$4,835.55
Grand Total.....	$213,926.90	$4,293.80	$7,508.76	$12,836.03	$55,876.88	$19,676.39

TABLE X
Annual Financial Statement of City E

	Total	High	School A	School B	School C	Evening School
Salaries.............	$115,101.88	$23,667.12	$8,769.38	$6,835.28	$6,235.83	$1,825.00
Fuel................	5,916.27	728.62	569.57	409.42	319.25	
Janitors' Supplies.....	717.47	45.13	67.08	62.95	49.22	1.46
Disinfectants.........	963.50	119.75	86.75	64.25	64.25	
Telephones..........	339.41	29.00	29.00	21.00	29.00	
Laundry.............	89.78	7.42	8.90	12.76	6.54	
Stationery Supplies...	2,536.90	453.42	210.33	188.81	165.93	
Drawing Supplies.....	645.50	6.89	88.82	55.21	52.13	
Kindergarten Supplies.	604.32		42.77	44.05	56.30	
Library Supplies......	319.16	98.90	27.94	11.83	16.69	
Apparatus...........	386.88	284.93	28.75	2.70	5.75	
Text-books..........	2,625.30	29.05	307.88	238.90	244.02	
Printing and Advertising................	423.76	53.21	30.75		20.20	18.75
(†) Pianos and Organs, Tuning, Etc.......	276.25	10.50	14.50	14.50	14.50	
Druggist's Supplies...	6.69		.42		.56	
Music Supplies.......	14.40		3.84	2.80	2.59	
Rent of Chairs.......	41.80	6.80	2.80		5.00	
Hectographs.........	40.90	16.40	5.70		1.70	
Miscellaneous Expenses	2,392.24	389.69	24.63	35.34	24.95	1.01
Total..........	$133,442.41	$25,946.83	$10,319.81	$7,999.80	$7,314.41	$1,846.22

TABLE X—Continued

	Domestic Science	Drawing	Physical Training	Music (*)	Truancy	Enumeration	Administration and General
Salaries.............	$912.87	$1,766.82	$800.00	$1,396.50	$196.60	$314.70	
Fuel................							
Janitors' Supplies.....							
Disinfectants.........							
Telephones..........							$39.41
Laundry.............	6.20						
Stationery Supplies...							369.97
Drawing Supplies.....							15.37
Kindergarten Supplies..							66.44
Library Supplies......	2.96						14.42
Apparatus...........							7.00
Text-books..........							612.42
Printing and Advertising	16.55						253.25
(†) Pianos and Organs, Tuning, Etc.........							
Druggist's Supplies....							
Music Supplies........							
Rent of Chairs........							
Hectographs..........		.90	2.40				
Miscellaneous Expenses		285.23	100.44	30.00			559.99
Total..........	$1,223.81	$1,868.16	$832.40	$1,396.50	$196.60	$314.70	$6,541.42

(*) $112.00 for text-books in music are included under text-books.
(†) Includes $85 for purchasing pianos.

TABLE XI—ANNU

	TOTAL	HIGH SCHOOL A	HIGH SCHOOL B	HIGH SCHOOL C	MANUAL TRAINING HIGH	SCHOOL A	SCHOOL B	
Repairs to Property and Buildings	$3,565.62	$306.69			$10.42	$4.02	$68.18	$16
Furniture and Fixtures	967.58	191.67						4
Repairs Furniture and Fixtures	2,702.92	458.84			10.32	63.46	208.35	8
Fire Alarm	656.22	112.09						
Teachers' Salaries	244,991.98		$19,786.50	$31,512.92	4,157.67	2,834.34	2,792.30	5,58
Janitors' Salaries	25,004.67	4,304.00				386.00	480.00	70
Labor	2,974.71	310.35			24.92	11.17	22.57	2
School House Improvement	8,590.16	738.32			4.10	18.74	14.06	2,35
Washing Towels	365.72	55.12				4.60	8.00	1
Heat	10,472.91	1,457.50			13.40	224.25	110.50	21
Light and Power	1,297.58	547.04			253.18	.24		
Telephones	541.05		26.25	32.79				2
Shoveling Snow	209.82	68.65					2.67	
Binding Books	271.74			86.44				
Text-books	10,476.32		1,376.70	723.18		62.35	50.33	18
Stock—Furniture and Fixtures	150.24	19.08				3.64	6.72	
Printing	617.70		6.00	57.80		.08	.60	
Teachers' and Pupils' Supplies	5,724.10		241.40	1,215.37	1.41	235.57	51.32	12
Janitors' Supplies	865.67	115.97			2.81	18.10	23.46	2
Miscellaneous	781.47							
Total	$321,228.18	$8,685.32	$21,436.85	$33,628.50	$4,478.23	$3,866.58	$3,839.06	
Laboratory Supplies	433.39	82.17	82.17	351.22				
Expenses	124.12	1.40	1.40	33.67	30.70			
Clerical Service	774.32	380.00	380.00	394.32				
Electrical Supplies	347.49			347.49				
Laboratory Services	87.00			87.00				
Domestic Science	74.19			74.19				
Express	496.21			2.36				
Lumber	632.81				401.68			
Hardware	508.79				360.76			
Supplies	273.20				12.38			
Groceries	274.86							
Milk	27.36							
Insurance	60.00							
Ice	15.92							
Salaries	3,731.40							
Superintendent's Salary	3,000.00							
Truant Officer's Salary	1,200.00							
Assistant Truant Officer's Salary	700.00							
Evening Truant Officer's Salary	30.00							
School House Mechanic's Salary	1,200.00							
Kindergarten Teacher's Salary	250.00							
Electric Labor	28.50							
Transportation of Officers	186.68							
Commitment of Truants	2,566.13							
Keep of Horse	456.15							
Kindergarten Supplies	.57							
Drawing Supplies	558.09							
Assistant Superintendent's Salary	1,520.19							
Advertising	94.51							
Graduation Expense	527.91							
Pensions	75.00							
Census	716.43							
Special Teachers' Salaries	5,523.75							
Text-books Sold	61.99							
Supplies Sold	13.79							
Annual Report	415.85							
Tuition	102.27							
Total	$27,088.87	$8,685.32	$463.57	$1,290.25	$805.52			
Grand Total	$348,317.05	$8,685.32	$21,900.42	$34,918.75	$5,283.75	$3,866.58	$3,839.06	

Statement of City W

Office	Supply Room	Work-Shop	Summer Annex	Grammar Manual Training	School W	New Chatham	Evening Drawing	Evening Elementary	Evening Grammar	Evening High
$25.00	$14.50	$55.94	$67.00							
....	....	....	18.00	$1,027.75	$287.50		$1,145.00	$1,911.50	$2,368.00	$1,715.00
....	....	....	4.00		28.00		170.00	195.00	260.00	328.00
....	.37	333.39	11.75	....	3.43	$69.95				
....	....	168.00								
....	....	10.96								
62.35	43.29	37.16	....	....	....	...	....	....	....	....
....	....	....	23.21	....	2.40	....	....	10.00	220.81	34.56
....	....	....	.58	....	....	....	7.50			
30.85	....	....	....	....	....	....	7.50	27.25	24.75	8.75
....	....	....	8.36	2.90	3.65					
....	1.95	.24	.08							
....	....	....	10.67	....	245.00					
$118.20	$60.11	$602.69	$143.65	$1,030.65	$569.98	$69.95	$1,322.50	$2,143.75	$2,873.56	$2,086.31
.65	16.31	2.00	....	....	....		3.80	.90	18.10	7.09
....	485.85	8.00								
....	....	231.13								
....	....	148.03								
33.54	16.62	....	....	....	....	....	....	23.14	33.46	44.32
....	60.00									
2,831.40	900.00									
$2,865.59	$1,478.78	$389.16	....	....	....		$3.80	$24.04	$51.56	$51.41
$2,983.79	$1,538.89	$991.85	$143.65	$1,030.65	$569.98	$69.95	$1,326.30	$2,167.79	$2,925.12	$2,137.72

CHAPTER V

AMOUNTS SPENT BY TWENTY CITIES FOR THE EDUCATION OF EACH PUPIL IN AVERAGE DAILY ATTENDANCE

Together with all the other data gathered there were obtained from each city figures showing the average daily attendance for all schools, for each class of schools, and for each school, in so far as such figures were available. There are given here the average daily attendance for all schools, for high schools, and for elementary schools in each of the twenty cities of which the financial statements have been printed.

TABLE XII
AVERAGE DAILY ATTENDANCE ON ALL SCHOOLS, ELEMENTARY SCHOOLS, AND HIGH SCHOOLS IN TWENTY CITIES

City	Total Attendance	High School	Elementary	Other Schools
City F	2,601.1	326.3	2,274.8	
City C	6,246	717	5,529	
City J	2,275	237	2,038	
City N	6,102.7	588.4	5,514.3	
City L	1,322	382	940	
City R	1,048.6	177.9	870.7	
City T	2,296	277	2,019	
City W	9,770	1,117	8,653	
City A	6,194.8	826.9	5,367.9	
City D	2,559.4	531.5	2,027.9	
City G	3,005	552	2,453	
City V	4,910	615	4,295	
City U	2,255	330	1,925	
City S	3,311	351	2,960	
City P	3,866	532	3,334	
City M	2,202.4	193.1	2,009.7	
City B	2,856.9	486	2,370.9	
City E	4,134.8	371.5	3,763.3	
City K	8,156	837	7,319	
City H	11,547	916	10,523	Training S., 66 Trade School, 42

Table XIII gives the expenditure per pupil in average daily attendance for each of the items of expenditure contained in the financial statements of the twenty cities listed. The results were obtained by dividing the amount of each item by the total number of pupils in average daily attendance as given in Table XII.

The unit used in measuring the cost of evening schools is the average daily attendance upon day schools—not a proper unit of measurement for that service. The average nightly attendance upon evening schools is the unit that should have been used. But the number of pupils in average nightly attendance was not obtainable from every city. Why it was not desired by the school superintendents is a mystery. Perhaps in New York State it was because the State Department of Education did not ask for such figures. The only proper unit of measurement common to all cities is pupil in average daily attendance. Therefore this unit was used.

TABLE XIII—Amounts Spent per Pupil in Average Daily Attendance on the Schools of Twenty Cities

City	F	C	J	N	L	R	T	W	A	D	G	V	U	S	P	M	B	E	K	H
Objects of Expenditure																				
Board of Education												1.00								
Clerk—Secretary of Board		.19	.26			.12		.38					.18		.35	.09	.18		.25	.88
Secretary, Business Manager and Clerks											1.33									
Other Employees							4.19		.39										.77	
Office and Miscellaneous		.08																		
Superintendent of Buildings																			.26	
Carpenter																	.36			
School Mechanic								.12												
Transportation of Officers								.02												
Keep of Horse								.05												
Census								.07								.0005				
Compulsory Education					.30									.33			.31			
Compulsory Education—Salaries		.12				.41		.20	.12						.22	2.38	.05		.23	
Truant Officers and Janitors				2.60																
Care of Truants							.0009	.26	.05											
Superintendent		.48				1.84		.31				.76			.67		1.05		.43	.57
Assistant Superintendent								.16												
Clerk and Superintendent														.66						
Stenographer		.08																		

City	F	C	J	N	L	R	T	W	A	D	G	V	U	S	P	M	B	E	K	H
Objects of Expenditure																				
Expenses of Superintendent																.09				
Superintendent and Supervising Principals									3.21											
Superintendent and Teachers				22.29	36.48											30.06				
Legal Services																.07				
Assessment Roll																.03				
Assessment and Taxes																.10				
Printing			.16	.07				.06	.07					.18	.16		.24			.25
Board Printing		.02																		
High School Printing		.03																		
Ward School Printing		.02																		
Printing Annual Report								.04												
Printing, Stationery and Postage						.29	.46													
Printing and Advertising										.19										
Advertising								.01								.14		.10		
Bill Posting																.007				
Express				.04				.05	.03											
Freight and Cartage																				
Freight, Cartage and Express									.002							.07			.18	.13
Postage																.01				

TABLE XIII—Continued

City	F	C	J	N	L	R	T	W	A	D	G	V	U	S	P	M	B	E	K	H
OBJECTS OF EXPENDITURE																				
Teachers' Retirement Fund..												.84					.81			
Pensions..								.007					.36			.30				
Salaries..										30.00								27.86		
Supervisors..									.65											
Supervisor of Music..		.20																		
Supervisor of Drawing..		.08																		
Principals..												4.65								
Teachers..	21.42	20.12	30.45				22.67	25.08			54.38	28.07	25.78	22.16	29.98		22.82			32.52
Regular Teachers..						19.75			22.68										24.58	
Substitute Teachers..						.01			.80										.87	
High School Teachers..	7.50																			
Evening Schools..				.50	.16	.15			.88				.50		.37				.39	1.10
Evening School Teachers..		.13															.35			
Drawing School..									.11											
Industrial Education..				.65				.57												.56
Special Teachers..													.56							
Teachers of Manual Training			3.04			.46													.63	
Manual Training Fund..									.006											
Teachers of Music..						.30													.16	
Teachers of Drawing..						.64													.24	

Amounts Spent by Twenty Cities for Education

CITY	F	C	J	N	L	R	T	W	A	D	G	V	U	S	P	M	B	E	K	H
OBJECTS OF EXPENDITURE																				
Teachers of Domestic Science						.57														
Teachers of Elocution						.10														
Vocational Teachers																			.19	
Truant Teachers		.07																		
Teachers of Penmanship																			.12	
Kindergarten Teachers						1.51		.03											1.44	
Open Air Class											.76									
Laboratory Service								.008												
Tuition		.05						.01		.01										.66
Tuition at Orphan Home								.08												
School Clerks			.61																	
Books																1.06				1.07
Text-books		.40		1.02		.33	.24	1.07	.85		1.28	1.25			1.04		1.08	.63	.12	
Binding Books								.03	.08											
Books and Supplies										2.34				2.34						
Books, Stationery and Supplies													3.30							
Supplies			1.81	1.10		.86		.03							1.01	1.03	.88			1.27
School Supplies							.30												1.21	
Teachers' and Pupils' Supplies								.59												

TABLE XIII—Continued

City: Objects of Expenditure	F	C	J	N	L	R	T	W	A	D	G	V	U	S	P	M	B	E	K	H
Stationery Supplies																		.61		
Stationery and Supplies											2.55									
Maps and Globes									.03											
Night School Supplies		.002																		
Manual Training Supplies						.04			.14				.74	.20						
Manual Training Material			.56																.02	
Domestic Science Supplies						.006		.007	.03											
Music Supplies																		.003		
Laboratory Supplies								.04												
Science Supplies									.03											
Sewing									.01					.003				.16		
Drawing Supplies								.06												
Drawing Material									.16									.15		
Kindergarten Supplies								.00006												
Druggist's Supplies																		.002		
Blanks									.05											
Busy Work									.02											
Erasers									.01											
Ink									.01											
Paper									.30											
Pens									.02											

City	F	C	J	N	L	R	T	W	A	D	G	V	U	S	P	M	B	E	K	H
Objects of Expenditure																				
Pencils									.02											
Flags									.01											
Lumber								.06												
Hardware								.05												
Groceries								.03												
Milk								.003												
Ice								.002												
Sundry Supplies									.06							.64				
Stationery, etc.												.44								
Supplies and Repairs		.61																		
Apparatus		.04				.04	.05											.09		
Hectographs																		.001		
Typewriters									.06											
Apparatus and Reference Books																.06				
Janitors			2.29					2.56	2.56		5.61	2.66	2.29	1.94	2.61		1.70		2.65	2.69
Janitors and Labor		1.88																		
Labor						2.40		.30	.10											
Janitors and Janitors' Supplies																			.32	
Laundry								.04								.05		.02		
Shoveling Snow								.02												

TABLE XIII—Continued

City	F	C	J	N	L	R	T	W	A	D	G	V	U	S	P	M	B	E	K	H
OBJECTS OF EXPENDITURE																				
Janitors' Tools and Supplies							.004													
Water, Janitors' Supplies, etc.												2.83								
Janitors' Supplies								.09	.13									.17	.17	.12
Towels and Soap									.05									.23		
Disinfectants																				
Heat								1.06												
Fuel		.12		1.32	3.10					2.50	2.70				2.49	.78		1.43	1.91	1.55
Fuel and Light						2.65								1.67			1.56			
Heat, Light and Power			3.62				1.74					1.87								
Fuel, Light and Water													1.24							
Water, Lighting and Power				.33																
Light															.37				.35	.18
Gas									.01											.27
Electricity		.10																		
Gas and Electricity								.13			.90					.05				
Light and Power									.19											
Electric Light and Power								.04												
Electrical Supplies									.13						.08	.07				
Water					.59	.55	.13							.92						
Repairs	6.21	.68	2.36	1.41						.39	1.57				1.92	.43	1.83		1.43	1.80
Repairs of Buildings						11.64	.67													

Amounts Spent by Twenty Cities for Education

Objects of Expenditure	F	C	J	N	L	R	T	W	A	D	G	V	U	S	P	M	B	E	K	H
Buildings and Repairs													1.16							
Repairs to Property and Buildings								.36												
Maintenance of Grounds															.35					
Repairs—Fences, Lawns, Walks, etc.							.15												.09	
Repairs to Furniture and Fixtures								.28												
Repairs to Apparatus								.003							.44					
Electric Labor									.03			2.21						.07		
Piano Care																				
Pianos, Organs, Tuning, etc.											.01					.01				
Clock Care																				
Repairs and Insurance	.15		.39			.47	.63	.006			.01		.17		.41	.01	.24		.63	.31
Insurance																				
Rent			.45								.30				.21				.05	.03
Leases	.02																			
Rent of Hall, Annual Meeting																.009				
Rent of Chairs																				
Medical Inspection			.31		.18						.78		.33							
School Nurse																	.10	.01		
Library	.26		.09		.40	.53	.48		.10			2.72	.07	.43					.17	

TABLE XIII—Concluded

CITY: Objects of Expenditure	F	C	J	N	L	R	T	W	A	D	G	V	U	S	P	M	B	E	K	H
School Libraries							.01													.05
Library Rent						.49									.06					
Library Salaries														.79						
Library Supplies																		.08		.04
Summer Schools																				
Play Grounds and Vacation Schools																	.15			
Summer Schools and Summer Gardens									.04	.29										
Transportation of Pupils			.20						.06											.30
Telephones	.							.05	.06				.13			.08		.08		.10
Graduation Expense	5.89			.28	4.69	1.79	.53	.08		.78	2.53		.25	.44	.89		1.06	.58	.23	.10
Miscellaneous Expense								.01												
New School Buildings			12.36								16.61	11.29		9.45		14.00	10.53			
Permanent Improvements											2.72									
School House Improvements							.23	.88												
School Houses New and Improved																				
Manual Training Plant			.31																	
Real Estate			8.77											3.37						
Sites		7.14					.													
Improvement of Grounds		.03																		

30 School Costs and School Accounting

Amounts Spent by Twenty Cities for Education

City	F	C	J	N	L	R	T	W	A	D	G	V	U	S	P	M	B	E	K	H
Objects of Expenditure																				
Sites and Permanent Improvements						.03													.02	
Furniture			.57	.05		.46			.16	.06	2.78			2.63	.47		.22		.16	.28
New Furniture																.64				
High School Furniture and Equipment (Spec. Appropriation)										10.41										
Furniture — New and Repaired							.26													
Furniture, Etc.	.40																			
Furniture and Apparatus											1.05									
Furniture and Fixtures								.11												
Fire Alarm								.07												
Drinking Fountains									.02											
Pictures		.008																		
Interest					1.00							4.61	.76			3.40				
Interest and Insurance														.08						
Bonds					4.53							1.43	1.10			7.20				
Bonds and Interest	2.95					4.74														
Text-books Sold								.006												
Supplies Sold								.001												
New Schools—Returned Interest													.46							
Grand Total	45.01	32.83	68.59	31.66	51.45	53.14	32.50	35.65	34.53	39.21	98.51	57.72	50.66	47.89	44.10	93.27	45.51	32.27	40.28	46.83

CHAPTER VI

PROBLEM ONE: COST PER PUPIL IN AVERAGE DAILY ATTENDANCE ON ALL SCHOOLS

Our first task as stated in the original purpose of the investigation is to learn the standard cost for public education for each pupil in average attendance on "All Schools." For convenience's sake we repeat in Table XIV the total expended for public education for each pupil in average attendance as given for each of the twenty cities listed in Table XII.

TABLE XIV

TOTAL EXPENDITURES PER PUPIL IN AVERAGE DAILY ATTENDANCE ON ALL SCHOOLS

City	Amount
City G	$98.51
City M	93.27
City J	68.49
City V	57.72
City R	53.14
City L	51.45
City U	50.66
City S	47.89
City H	46.83
City B	45.51
City F	45.01
City P	44.10
City K	40.27
City D	39.21
City W	35.65
City A	34.53
City C	32.83
City T	32.50
City E	32.27
City N	31.66

From Table XIV we find that the total expended per pupil varies from $31.66, in City N, to $98.51, in City G. The average amount expended per pupil was $50.68. The median expenditure per pupil was $45.26, while the mode was $32.00. The average deviation from the median is $12.27.

That City G should spend in one year approximately three times as much per pupil for education as another city, seems remarkable. Why should one city spend 32 per cent as much as another for performing, presumably, the same service? But is the presumption correct that the expenditures are in payment of the same services?

The answer to this question can be learned from the heading of the last table, which states that it contains the *expenditures* per pupil in average daily attendance. In the discussion preceding, we have used the terms expended and spent in speaking of amounts of money stated as used for purposes of education.

When these cities were visited it was for the purpose of learning the *costs* of education for the last financial year. From not one city could such costs be obtained. No city knew how much the performance of this service of education had cost it. This was because, instead of accounting for the revenue accrued and the expense incurred during such year, account was kept only of the funds received and the funds expended, so that the statements preceding are accurate statements of cost only in so far as it happens that none of the liabilities incurred during the year preceding that under consideration is met out of the funds of the latter year and in so far as it happens that none of the expenditures of the year considered are for expense to be incurred in the year following, i.e., in so far as it happens that the liabilities incurred during the year under consideration are met out of such year's appropriations. To what extent the expenditures listed are for services and things received during the period stated is not known.

Thus there may have been some supplies and text-books ordered by the school board of City C in the spring of 1910, a part of which were distributed to the pupils and used during that time, yet they were not paid for until the early part of 1911 out of the 1911 appropriations. Or there may have been ordered some supplies and text-books during 1911 that were received in that year and were paid for out of the appropriations for same year; but they may not have been distributed for use in any part of 1911. The cost of such supplies and text-books in no way enters into the cost of education during 1911 because they were not used during that period.

Again, some supplies and text-books may have been purchased in 1911; they may have been distributed to the schools during that year; but in the case of supplies they may not all have been consumed during that period and some of the text-books may be in condition to be used during a part or all of 1912. The value of the supplies not used and of the text-books for further use do not enter into the cost of education in 1911 because they were used in 1912.

The same is true for all the other items of expenditure. No city knew its cost of education; each knew only how much had been spent for that service. All of which means that the original purpose of this investigation could not be accomplished because of the first great defect in the data obtained revealing the same defect in the method of accounting for school funds. The defect is this:

> *No attempt is made to account for revenue accruing and expense incurred for education during any given period, accounts being kept so as to show only receipts and expenditures.*

Study of the financial statements reveals a second reason for the great variation in school expenditures for one year. Thus City F spent $1,028.29 for furniture, etc. Did the furniture, etc., purchased with this sum replace some old furniture, etc., that had worn out? Did it purchase some new furniture, etc., that was to be used in addition to that already in use? Or was part for the first purpose and part for the second? Again City W spent $1,117.82 for furniture and fixtures. Did the $1,117.82 purchase new furniture and fixtures to be used in place of old or in addition to that already in use?

Our data show City F spent $17,148.36 for repairs, and not one cent for improvements; that City C spent $4,249.65 for repairs, $44,613.22 for sites, and $171.44 for improvement of grounds, and not one cent for improving buildings. City J spent $5,375.24 for repairs, $28,108.20 for new school buildings, $705.53 for manual training plant, $19,950 for real estate, and not one cent for improvement of buildings, unless it be that part used by the manual training plant. One could go through the list of cities and he would find only City T, City W, and City G that account for expenditures for purposes of improving the school plant as distinct from expenditures for repairs and replacement. Thus we find included in the expenditures given for running the schools during the period chosen expenditures both for maintenance and for capital outlay. But expenditures for capital outlay should not be included in the expenditures necessary for running the school plant. Capital outlay has for its purpose the accommodation of many other pupils than those attending during the year under consideration, and therefore expenditures for capital outlay should not be treated as a part of the expenditures for pupils now in attendance only.

Again, Table XIII shows expenditures for repairs in City R to be $11.64 per pupil, in City F $6.21, in City P $2.71, in City A $0.03. That is, from the data available one city spent 488 per cent as much for repairs as another.

These conditions show the second defect in the data obtained, revealing the same defect in the method of accounting for school funds. Every productive concern must expend money to repair parts of its equipment and structures. Unless the value of the equipment and structures has been decreased on the books in proportion to the decrease in actual value, these expenditures are to be charged to the running expenses of the concern. Every productive concern must likewise expend money for new equipment and sometimes new structures to take the place of old. If the equipment and structures replaced are carried at their old value on the books, these expenditures are likewise a part of the running expenses. Every growing concern must expend money for new equipment and new structures that are in addition to those already in use. These increase the permanent value of the plant. These expenditures may not be made because of the product that is being turned out now but because of the product to be turned out in the future. So the expenditures cannot be charged to the objects now being produced, but must be charged to the objects to be produced in the future. That is, every productive concern has found it necessary to keep account of expenditures for maintenance distinct from those for capital outlay. The second defect, then, that destroys for the purpose of the investigation the data obtained is this:

There is no attempt to distinguish expenditures made to enable education to be carried on with present facilities, from expenditures made to increase facilities for education, i. e., there is no attempt to distinguish expenditures for maintenance from expenditures for capital outlay.

Examination of the data in the preceding tables has shown (1) that, for the items of cost concerning which information is desired, it is impossible to get information concerning the *cost* of any of them, (2) that if we look for the total expenditures per pupil for running the schools for one year we cannot obtain such information because such expenditures have not been distinct from expenditures for new buildings and equipment, or for improvements of the same. That is, stated again, we cannot get (1) the total cost per unit for education for one year in each city, or (2) the total expenditures per unit for education for one year in each city. As shown in the statement of our purpose, the next items of cost desired are the total cost per pupil for each kind of school, i.e., for all elementary schools, for all high schools, for all vocational schools, for all evening schools.

CHAPTER VII

PROBLEM TWO: COST PER PUPIL IN AVERAGE DAILY ATTENDANCE ON EACH KIND OF SCHOOL

We can say at once, as was shown above, that we cannot get the total *cost* per unit for each kind of school, since account is kept only of expenditures; so that, immediately, the only accurate basis of comparison is lacking. But again, as before, we can attempt to learn the total expended per pupil for each kind of school. Examination with this end in view shows the following with regard to each city:

City F spent for high school teachers, $19,515.77. No other information is given concerning expenditures for each kind of school. The one item above is worth little because we do not know whether it includes expenditures for salaries and wages for high school principal, for supervisors, for teachers, for janitors and labor, or includes expenditures for teachers only or for some combination of the above. Nothing in the other information contained in the statement of City F helps us to understand what this item contains. That is, this city gives no information that can be used to learn the expenditure for each kind of school.

City C gives more information. This city spent the amount shown in Table XV.

TABLE XV

AMOUNTS SPENT FOR EACH KIND OF SCHOOL AS SHOWN IN THE STATEMENT FROM CITY C

	HIGH SCHOOL	ELEMENTARY SCHOOLS	EVENING SCHOOLS
Teachers	$25,526.50	$100,153.39	$792.00
Fuel	23.83	731.23	
Janitors and Labor	1,711.59	9,975.09	
Supplies and Repairs	767.41	3,038.82	
Printing	178.56	144.89	
Supplies			11.65

The only item not clear here is teachers. Without doubt, however, it includes personal services for administration, i.e., the principals' salaries, as well as for instruction. There is lacking, however, information concerning the amount spent by the high school distinct from that spent by elementary schools for supervision of music, for supervision of drawing, for gas and electricity, for insurance, for pictures, for text-books, and for apparatus; while no information is given concerning expenditures for evening schools except the above for teachers and supplies. Yet the evening schools were held in the high school or elementary school buildings or both; and so part of the expenditures for fuel, janitors and labor, and supplies and repairs expended for high and elementary schools should be charged against evening schools. It can hardly be possible that but one evening school even can be charged with only $11.65 for supplies for a season, let alone two or more evening schools. The only information furnished by City C that we can use is the expenditures for teachers.

City J gives no information whatever concerning the expenditures for each kind of school. It is apparently one of the cities that cares not enough for the proper provision of educational opportunity to find out how much is spent for giving the majority of pupils an elementary education in comparison with the amount spent for secondary education in comparison with the amount spent for vocational education (except for manual training) in comparison with the amount spent for evening school instruction; but apparently does care greatly to know how much is spent for teachers in comparison with the amount spent for janitors' wages in comparison with the amount spent for secretary of the board of education in comparison with the amount spent for printing, and so forth. City J is doubtless one of the cities that wishes only to use its accounts to insure the faithfulness of its representatives by making them account for the amounts appropriated for education.

There is an interesting condition revealed in the statement of City J, however. Education has long been considered as one great service; expenditures had to be made for various objects in order that the one great service could be performed. So accounts were kept of amounts spent for the various objects, as teachers, fuel, etc. Then manual training was introduced into the curriculum. This was a distinct subdivision of the great service, education; that it was distinct and was a subdivision of education is shown by the fact that it was introduced so late in the development of education. And like all new things we purchase, whether as individuals or organizations, the cost had to be considered. So City J did and does now account for the expenditures that it makes for personal service, for material, and for the plant to instruct pupils in manual training. Is there any more reason why City J should account for the expenditures for instruction in manual training than for instruction in reading the English language, in writing it, in arithmetic, in each or any of the other subjects of instruction?

In City N, the ninth grade of the elementary schools is housed in the high school building. So of the amounts spent for janitors, for water, light, fuel and repairs, the amount to be charged to the high school is not known. However, we do learn that there was spent for

	High School	Elementary Schools	Evening Schools
Teachers	$22,292.26	$110,744.42	$2,978.00
Furniture	22.87	312.08	
Text-books	2,049.82	4,177.69	4.95
Supplies	1,469.72	5,149.58	83.68

City L, like City J, accounts only for certain objects of expenditure, though it does state that $213.50 was spent for night school. What the amount includes we do not know.

City R has the beginning of a system of accounting that would serve her purposes fairly well if it were properly used. But by making the library, domestic science, and manual training divisions of the organization coördinate with the schools, and by including under general expense too many charges that should have been made to one or more of the divisions of organization, the usefulness of the system has been minimized. Thus we cannot learn the total expenditure for instruction in each kind of school because to general expense have been charged for

Teachers, Regular	$40.00
Teachers, Substitute	12.00
Teachers, Music	310.00
Teachers, Drawing	670.00
Teachers, Domestic Science	600.00
Teachers, Elocution	100.00
Free Text-books	246.63
Furniture	317.85
Supplies	459.85

The only items of current expense for which it is possible to get the amounts expended for each kind of school entirely distributed are

	High School	Elementary Schools
Kindergarten Teachers		$1,580.00
Water Tax	$288.03	288.04

The item of $288.03 for water tax for the high school and of $288.04 for water tax for School A, makes us at once ask on what basis the distribution of charges was made to the various divisions of the organization. Was the high school charged with half of the water tax because it used half the water, or because it has just as many pupils as School A, or because that was a convenient distribution to make? The high school and School A are connected, practically forming one building. In the building is included also the superintendent's office.

For City R we do find a somewhat more complete accounting of expenditures for night school as follows:

Teaching	$299.50
Repair of School Houses	19.07
Furniture	8.13
Fuel and Lighting	28.60
Janitors and Janitors' Supplies	6.24
Supplies	13.58
	$375.12

But, what is this information worth? Was only $13.58 spent for supplies for night school during the season? Were $6.24 sufficient to pay both for the services of a janitor or janitors and for janitor's supplies during the season? Were $8.13 and $19.07 sufficient to pay for the repair and replacement of furniture and of buildings due to carrying on the night school? It does not seem possible; these are without doubt only certain expenditures that could be charged directly to the night school. The only datum we would be warranted in using for City R is the amount spent for teaching in the night school.

City T states that there was spent for

	High School	Elementary Schools
Repair of Schoolhouses	$229.24	$1,298.18
Insurance	265.00	1,176.10
Repairs (Fences, Walks, Lawns, etc.)	19.23	326.64
Janitors' Tools and Supplies		9.80

These are probably accurate statements of the amounts spent for the objects named. Such accurate account, however, is kept of none of the other items, not even of salaries of teachers, which are most easily charged to the different schools. This is due to the fact that City T is divided into districts, each under a local board having charge of the care of the school house in its district but having no control over other expenditures, which are therefore not charged to the different schools.

City W has the most up-to-date and serviceable accounting system of the cities visited. Yet here, as in City R, such use is not made of the system as was probably intended. If it were used as it should be, not so many questions could be asked that it could not answer. The two defects are these: (1) manual training in the elementary schools and cooking are not charged to the schools in which they are taught, and (2) expenditures are charged to the general account that should be charged to the various schools. These are in addition to the defect common to all the cities, i.e., the accounting is not based on revenue and expense.

The statement from City W does, however, show accurately the amounts spent, as shown in Table XVI.

TABLE XVI

AMOUNTS SPENT FOR EACH KIND OF SCHOOL AS SHOWN IN THE STATEMENT FROM CITY W

	High School	Elementary Schools	Evening Schools
Repairs to Property and Buildings	$317.11	$3,248.51	
Furniture and Fixtures	191.67	593.79	
Repairs to Furniture and Fixtures	469.16	2,233.76	
Fire Alarm	112.09	544.13	
Teachers' Salaries	55,457.09	62,864.59	$7,139.50
Labor	335.27	2,293.93	
Washing Towels	55.12	310.60	
Heat	1,470.90	8,991.05	
Light and Power	800.22	497.36	
Shoveling Snow	68.65	141.17	
Binding Books	86.44	185.30	
Text-books	2,099.88	8,087.86	265.37
Stock, Furniture and Fixtures	19.08	130.00	
Teachers' and Pupils' Supplies	1,458.18	4,257.56	
Janitors' Supplies	118.78	744.62	
Laboratory Supplies	433.39		
Clerical Service	774.32		
Electrical Supplies	347.49		
Laboratory Service	87.00		
Domestic Science	74.19		
Express	2.36		
Lumber	401.68		
Hardware	361.33		
Supplies	12.38	109.74	100.92
Groceries for Cooking School		274.86	
Milk for Cooking School		27.36	
Ice for Cooking School		15.92	

The above is an accurate statement of expenditures for each kind of school except that it does not include $558.09 for drawing supplies and $5,523.75 for special teachers' salaries, both of which are charged to the general account. With these exceptions the above might be used for purposes of comparison.

City A has a form of statement, the purpose of which is to show periodically the amounts expended for each school and for administration for various objects. However, the tendency to charge to administration expenditures not quickly and easily chargeable to each school results in the form being of little help. Some examples are the following: Of $473.04 spent for binding books $459.34 is charged to administration. Of $74.33 spent for flags $39.02 is charged to administration. Of $381.42 spent for graduation $219.29 is charged to administration. Of $877.86 spent for manual training (other than personal service) $134.81 is charged to administration. Of $124.90 spent for busy work $42.77 is charged to administration. And of $199.02 spent for cooking (other than personal service) $199.02 is charged to administration. In the statement of the other expenditures we find the same defect. The statement of expenditures for personal service follows:

	High School	Elementary Schools	Administration	Total
Janitors...................	$5,322.29	$10,515.74		$15,838.03
Regular Teachers..........	41,021.17	98,922.43	$547.71	140,491.31
Substitute Teachers........	612.00	2,974.75	1,378.87	4,965.62
Superintendent and Supervising Principals..........	2,600.00	14,565.53	2,700.00	19,865.53
Truant Officers.............			725.00	725.00

Because some expenditures for substitute and for regular teachers are charged to administration one would be justified in using for comparison only the data given for janitors, superintendent and supervising principals.

Cities D, U, S, P, M, and B, like City J, give no information that one would be justified in using in making comparisons that are true and accurate, i.e., for comparing objects of expenditure that differ only in the amounts expended.

The statement of expenditures for City V may be accepted or rejected as desired, because its basis is not known, due to the fact that the superintendent of schools stated that he had no authority over the school finances and the secretary of the board of education, and because the secretary of the board was good enough to furnish the statement as given but not to allow examination of his books or his system of accounting. It would seem that the statement should be used in all respects as given, were it not for the notable coincidence that we find the expenditure for the high school library exactly one-tenth of the total. With the exception of this item one is warranted to use the data contained in the statement of City V.

For our purpose the usefulness of the data contained in the statement of City G is injured by two facts: (1) Some $16,000 was spent for the manual training department without showing how the expenditure was distributed between elementary and high school pupils; (2) $6,698.18 was spent for a central heating plant, which furnished heat to the high school, an elementary school, and the administration division, but there was no distribution of that expense. One is justified, however, in using certain of the data concerning the expenditures for night school, which were as follows:

Teachers' Salaries	$4,813.95
Janitors' Salaries	372.50
Stationery and Supplies	122.89
Free Text-books	28.22
Incidentals	71.64
Light and Power	63.79

City E spent for salaries for instruction in domestic science, drawing, physical training, and music $4,876.19 that is not distributed to the various schools. It does give the following information that we might use:

	High School	Elementary Schools	Evening Schools
Salaries			$1,825.00
Fuel	$728.62	$5,187.65	
Janitors' Supplies	45.13	670.88	1.46
Disinfectants	119.75	843.75	
Telephones	29.00	271.00	
Pianos and Organs, Tuning, etc.	10.50	265.75	
Druggists' Supplies		6.69	
Music		14.40	
Rent of Chairs	6.80	35.00	

City K uses the same system of accounting as City R; it has the same defects in that it charges too many expenditures to general expense and does not distribute its expenditures for manual training to the various schools. The information given in Table XVII was obtained from the statement:

TABLE XVII

AMOUNTS SPENT FOR EACH KIND OF SCHOOL AS SHOWN IN THE STATEMENT FROM CITY G

	VOCATIONAL SCHOOLS	EVENING SCHOOLS
Teachers．．．	$1,540.00	$3,208.00
Free Text-books．．		20.70
School Apparatus．．	53.00	
Repair of School Houses．．	401.31	
Insurance．．．	178.50	
Fences, Sidewalks, etc．．	14.25	
Printing, Stationery and Postage．．	10.50	7.50
Fuel．．．	29.50	
Lighting．．．	16.51	
Janitors．．．	416.66	87.00
Janitors' Supplies．．	1.78	
Miscellaneous．．	21.93	
School Supplies．．．	886.13	8.25

It may be asked what justification there is for giving these amounts as accurate statements of expenditures for the objects named, while there is not likewise given the amounts spent for elementary schools and high school. There is no justification except the feeling that these expenditures for vocational schools and evening schools are easier of identification and are less likely to be dropped into the general expense column, than is the case when expenditures must be distributed over many schools of the same kind.

For City H the data shown in Table XVIII are accurately charged but for the fact that the expenditures for elementary schools, unless it is stated to the contrary, include expenditures for a teachers' training school that uses a part of one of the elementary school buildings.

TABLE XVIII

AMOUNTS SPENT FOR EACH KIND OF SCHOOL AS SHOWN IN THE STATEMENT FROM CITY H

	HIGH SCHOOL	ELEMENTARY SCHOOLS	TRADE SCHOOL	TRAINING SCHOOL
Fuel	$1,498.00	$15,670.37	$779.20	
Transportation		984.90	488.23	
Furniture	772.69	2,473.38	3.35	$90.00
Printing	354.38	1,956.41	558.38	35.03
Books	3,620.38	4,034.66	161.33	252.95
Libraries	74.65	452.05		
Gas	561.00	1,536.10	20.70	
Electricity	271.76	1,711.37	1,084.60	
Rent		307.75		
Telephones	38.23	1,084.37	27.03	
Insurance	285.00	2,811.57	475.00	
Repairs	2,672.65	18,116.88	42.27	7.98
Janitors' Supplies	76.21	1,161.54	120.31	
School Clerks	1,675.00	6,280.00		
Teachers	62,430.17	296,920.39	13,570.70	2,608.00
Janitors	720.00	29,278.01	1,065.00	

Study of these twenty cities has shown a third defect in the data obtained revealing the same defect in the methods of accounting. This is the defect:

> *No city obtains the total expenditures for each kind of school, so that it is impossible to learn the totals expended for high schools, for elementary schools, for vocational schools, and for evening schools.*

This means that the second purpose of the investigation cannot be accomplished.

CHAPTER VIII

PROBLEM THREE: COST PER PUPIL IN AVERAGE DAILY ATTENDANCE FOR EACH CHARACTER OF SERVICE

The third purpose of the investigation was to learn the total cost per pupil in average daily attendance for each character of service performed in connection with education. These are administration, supervision, instruction, operation, maintenance, and capital outlay. These are each defined as follows:

Administration is used here in its usual sense to include all services performed for an organization as a whole or a division as a whole, not chargeable directly to any of the units that compose the organization or division. This includes the determination, direction, and inspection of work to be done or already accomplished in so far as none of such work is so specialized as to become a part of supervision. Thus the superintendent performs services that cannot be charged directly to high schools or elementary schools nor to manual training or arithmetic instruction. The same is true of the principal of a school who is thus the administrative head of a division.

Supervision includes all services whose purpose is to determine the work to be done, to give orders that work be done, and to see that work is done in the performance of the various functions of education, e.g., instruction in drawing, in reading, and in geography. Administration exists to perpetuate the educational organization, to keep it running with each part bearing to each other part the proper relations; it corresponds to line organization in the army and serves the same purpose. Supervision is the result of functional organization; it determines largely the efficiency of an institution. It means centralization of control over specialized functions throughout an organization. In the army the surgeon is in control, under the commanding officer and representing him, of the care of the health of the army. In the school organization the supervisor of drawing, under the superintendent and representing him, is in charge of the instruction in drawing for the purpose of making it as efficient as possible.

Instruction is direct production in education, i.e., it is the service that is performed directly upon the material, children, for whose development the organization exists.

Operation includes all services performed to provide the place in which the other services are performed. It includes the heating, cleaning, and ventilating of buildings and all that pertain to them.

Maintenance, as previously explained, includes all services and things necessary to keep the school plant in its present condition so that the present amount of administration, supervision, instruction, and operation may go on.

Capital outlay includes all services and things that are for the purpose of increasing the amount or improving the quality of administration, supervision, instruction and operation. Here, for example, is included a new boiler in addition to that already in use, the new addition being made to increase the comfort and therefore the amount of work that can be performed in the instruction of children.

Examination of the financial statements or of the summary table will show how much information can be obtained concerning each character of service. We already know two facts concerning them: (1) no costs are obtainable, and (2) there is no clear distinction between maintenance and capital outlay, making it impossible to get the information concerning the cost of the first. So we need examine the data only to learn the expenditures for administration, supervision, instruction and operation.

City F and City D record no expenditures for administration as distinct from other characters of expenditure. Cities J, L and U record an expenditure for personal service by the clerk of the school board or by the attendance officer with apparently no other expenditure for administrative purposes. Some cities like City R have charged to administration or general expense, not only all the expenditures made for it but also expenditures for teachers, text-books, and supplies, more than should be charged to it. City W has charged to the general account expenditures for kindergarten teacher, for special teachers, for drawing supplies, for graduation expense, and other items that should be charged to the schools. City A has charged to administration, expenditures for drawing material, graduation, manual training, sewing, busy work, cooking, regular teachers and substitute teachers, that should have been charged directly to the schools.

City V states that it spent $4,890.00 for the board of education and $3,740.60 for the superintendent; but it does not give the expenditures for anything other than personal service. City S gives the salary of the superintendent and clerk but no other information concerning administration. City E has charged to administration and general expense, expenditures for drawing supplies, kindergarten supplies, and text-books, that should have been charged to the various schools. City K has charged to general expense expenditures for teachers, text-books, school apparatus, school supplies and cooking supplies, that should be charged to the various schools. In City H there have been charged to general expense, expenditures for superintendents and for the clerk's office; what these include is not shown. All of which makes apparent the impossibility of a true comparison of expenditures for administration.

To the incompleteness and indefiniteness described above is to be added the fact that no city records for administration the share that it should bear of the operation and maintenance expense of the school buildings in which the administration offices are located. This omission makes the operation and maintenance expense for instruction greater, and the operation and maintenance expense for administration less, than it actually is. Thus it is found that a true comparison of the expenditures for school administration in twenty cities is impossible.

The information concerning expenditures for supervision is more meager than for administration. The statements from Cities R, W, E, and K give the amounts spent for salaries and wages for certain subjects as drawing, music, and penmanship, but do not state whether the salaries are in payment of personal services for supervision or instruction in such so-called special subjects. Only three cities, C, A, and V state the amounts spent for the service of persons employed as supervisors. From no city was there obtained any information concerning expenditures for various supplies and materials for supervision. Nor does any city state how much was spent for supervision by school principals. Thus from no city are the data available on which to base a comparison of expenditures for supervision.

The statements made above, concerning the deficiencies of the information of expenditures for administration and supervision, could be repeated here in criticism of the information concerning expenditures for instruction. For where data are lacking concerning expenditures for these two services, by so much are the data concerning expenditures for instruction inaccurate in being correspondingly too great. Thus "City F and City D record no expenditures for administration as distinct from other characters of expenditure" (p. 48). This means that the expenditures of City F for teachers' wages and high school teachers are inaccurate, at least to the degree that they include expenditures for administration. Likewise "the statements from Cities R, W, E, and K give the amounts spent for salaries and wages for certain subjects as drawing, music, and penmanship but do not state whether the salaries are in payment of personal services for supervision or instruction" (p. 49). "From no city was there obtained any information concerning the expenditures for supplies and materials and the various other services for supervision" (p. 49). By so much are the statements of expenditures for supplies and materials for instruction too great. Thus, as was the case with administration and with supervision, it is impossible to make a true comparison of expenditures for instruction.

In trying to learn the amounts expended for operation we have difficulties as follows:

City F gives no information concerning expenditures for operation.

City C accounts for no janitorial supplies.

City J accounts for $8,228.73 for heat, light and power, but for nothing else for operation.

City N accounts for fuel and for water, lighting and power. Expenditures for personal service are given with truant officers under the title, "truant officers and janitors."

City L accounts for fuel only.

City T accounts for no personal services for operation.

City G accounts only for janitors, for heat, for light and power.

City S accounts only for janitors, and for fuel and light.

City U accounts only for janitors and for fuel, light and water.

City P accounts only for janitors, for fuel, for light, and for water.

City M accounts only for laundry service, for fuel, for gas and electricity, and for water.

City B accounts only for janitors, and for fuel and light.

City E gives no information concerning cost of janitorial service.

For the remaining cities we get the information concerning their expenditures for operation as given in Table XIX.

TABLE XIX

AMOUNTS SPENT FOR OPERATION AS GIVEN IN THE STATEMENTS FROM SIX CITIES

	R	W	A	V	K	H
Janitor............		$25,004.67	$15,838.03	$13,093.04	$21,589.05	$31,063.01
Labor.............		2,974.71	640.50			
Janitors and Janitors' Supplies........	$2,513.48					
Laundry...........			365.72			
Shoveling Snow....			209.82			
Water, Janitors' Supplies, etc.......				13,886.82		
Janitors' Supplies....			865.67	824.13		1,354.47	1,358.06
Towels and Soap.....				311.16		
Disinfectants........						
Heat...............			10,472.91			
Fuel................					15,566.50	17,947.65
Fuel and Light......	2,775.05			9,181.62		
Light...............					2,892.80	
Gas................				78.84		2,117.80
Electricity..........						3,067.73
Light and Power.....		1,297.58				
Electric Light and Power...........				1,173.76		
Electrical Supplies...						
Water..............	576.07			777.72		
Total...........	$5,864.60	$41,538.57	$19,644.14	$36,161.48	$41,402.82	$55,554.25

We are able to compare for only these six cities the expenditures for operation. The number of course is insufficient, but it may be interesting to make the comparison as shown in Table XX.

TABLE XX

EXPENDITURE PER PUPIL IN AVERAGE DAILY ATTENDANCE FOR OPERATION OF SCHOOLS IN SIX CITIES

City R..................	$5.59	City V..................	$7.36
City W..................	4.35	City K..................	5.08
City A..................	3.17	City H..................	4.81

As was the case with administration, supervision, and instruction, so is it with operation; there are not sufficient data on which to base a true comparison of expenditures for the performance of that service.

Of the impossibility of learning expenditures for maintenance and capital outlay mention has already been made. Thus we are faced with the fourth defect in the data obtained indicating a like defect in the systems of accounting employed:

No city obtains the total expended for each character of expenditure, so that it is impossible to learn the totals spent for administration, supervision, instruction, operation, maintenance, and capital outlay.

CHAPTER IX

PROBLEM FOUR: COST PER PUPIL IN AVERAGE DAILY ATTENDANCE FOR PERSONAL SERVICE, SUPPLIES, AND VARIOUS SERVICES

The next purpose of the investigation was to determine the standard unit costs of education for certain objects of expense, viz., personal service, i.e., the service of persons whose time is placed at the disposal of the employer; supplies, i.e., those things that are consumed when used directly or indirectly for purposes of education; and various services, i.e., all expenditures for objects other than the two mentioned.

Examination of the statements obtained from the twenty cities shows the following concerning expenditures for personal service:

The statement from City F gives the amount spent for teachers and for high school teachers. Out of what fund the expenditures for other employees are made is not stated. It would seem strange for the superintendent's salary to be paid out of the contingent fund for it is hardly a contingent expense. The same is true of expenditures for janitors. Because City J has included an expenditure for medical inspection without stating how much of it is for supplies or other objects and how much is for personal service we are unable to learn the total expended for that object.

City N spent $3,066.63 for evening schools and $3,960.88 for industrial training, giving no information as to the amounts spent for personal service, supplies, and various services.

City L spent money for medical inspection, night school, and compulsory education, but in the statement from that city there is no information as to amounts spent for any objects.

City T spent $1,100.00 for a public library with no statement as to the services and things purchased.

City A stated that it expended $5,474.59 for evening schools, $686.29 for a drawing (evening) school and $650.11 for medical inspection, with no further information concerning the objects of the expenditures.

City G spent $2,370.75 for medical inspection, $1,819.20 for summer gardens and summer schools and $2,287.93 for an open-air class, but we cannot learn how much was spent for personal service, supplies, or other objects for any of them.

City V states that $13,370.00 was spent for library purposes. Whether the expenditure was for books for school libraries or was for a library used primarily for school pupils is not evident, nor the amount spent for personal service, etc., if the latter was the case.

Evening schools and medical inspection are stated by City U as having had money expended for them though for what objects the money was spent there is no information.

The same condition is found in the statement of City S for compulsory education; of City B for playgrounds and vacation schools; and of City H for summer schools ($428.98), industrial education ($6,421.97) and for evening schools ($12,737.13).

Thus of the twenty cities studied only Cities C, R, W, *D*, P, M, E, and K give in the financial statements presented the amounts expended for the service of persons employed by their school boards. There are not enough cities to make comparison more than interesting. Table XXI shows the total cost per pupil for personal service in these cities.

TABLE XXI

AMOUNTS SPENT PER PUPIL IN AVERAGE DAILY ATTENDANCE FOR PERSONAL SERVICE FOR EDUCATION IN EIGHT CITIES

City	Amount
City C	$23.33
City R	26.34
City W	29.80
City D	30.08
City P	33.83
City M	32.53
City E	27.84
City K	33.21

The same cause that prevents a comparison of expenditures for personal service prevents a comparison of expenditures for supplies. That is, twelve of the cities include in their statements expenditures for the performance of certain services, which expenditures have not been analyzed to show for what objects they were made. Of the remaining cities we find that City C gives together the expenditures for supplies and repairs; City R gives together the expenditures for janitors and janitors' supplies; City D gives together books and supplies. From only four statements can it be learned how much was spent for supplies.

It would be a simple matter to obtain the amounts spent for other objects than personal service and supplies by subtracting from the total expenditures of each city the amounts expended for these objects. But we have shown that the statements do not tell accurately the amounts expended for these two objects; so that, even if the totals given were accurate statements of expenditure, the results would not be comparable. And when we remember that the total expenditures as given in the statements include expenditures for capital outlay indistinguishable from those for running the schools during the year under consideration, we realize more the worthlessness of such a comparison.

The uselessness of the data in the financial statements for learning the amounts expended for personal service, supplies, and various services for administration, supervision, instruction, operation, and maintenance has been shown in our discussion of expenditures for those characters of expenditure. The same indefiniteness, incompleteness, and overlapping were found as have been found throughout the discussion. This reveals a fifth defect of the data, indicating a like defect in the method of accounting:

> *There is no common classification of objects of expenditure, by which may be described the expenditures for all schools, for each kind of school, and for each character of expenditure.*

PART II. A STUDY OF SCHOOL ACCOUNTING

CHAPTER X

DESCRIPTION AND USE OF DOCUMENTS OF EXPENDITURE

In the preceding pages there have been listed specific defects that make worthless for our purpose the data of school expenditures obtained from twenty cities. These defects can be summarized in the one sentence:

School administrative officers exercise practically no administrative control through the financial details of their business.

This statement is justified when we consider the administrative function. Administration of education is a distinct service just as education itself is. Administration is one of the divisions of the large function, education. The service rendered in administration is the decision as to work to be done, the ordering of work to be done and the inspection of work done. The action of administrative officers is determined by the information they receive concerning work done. In education such information has come from first-hand visits of administrative officers and from pupils' records. To a relatively small degree have actions of administrative officers depended upon information of financial details. This has been due generally to the superintendents themselves. Their attitude is shown by the statement of one of their number that he "was employed to look after the education of the city's children; the treasurer of the board was chosen to look after the money." It is interesting to note that the expenditures per pupil for education in this city were among the highest of the twenty cities listed. That is, this superintendent, because, as we frankly believe, he regarded as his function the administration of the training of his city's children with little regard to expenditures, was able to supply but one-half or two-thirds the training that he could have supplied if he had given but a little more attention to his city's school finances. The manager of an industrial concern would not very long pay $75 for a service that he could purchase for $50 or less. Nor will it always be true that a school superintendent can spend $75 per pupil for education when the same can be furnished for $50 or less. Instead of being continually anxious to know how much has been spent for teachers, for supplies, and the like, as has heretofore been the case, successful superintendents will be continually anxious to know how much teaching has been obtained for this expenditure, how much instruction in literature did this expenditure purchase, and the like.

In order that it may be used to accomplish the purposes for which it exists, accounting must record certain classes of information. The three principal classes of facts are: data describing transactions with outsiders to which the organization is a party; data describing transactions between various divisions within the organization; and data summarizing and relating these transactions. That is, in its simplest form, accounting requires records of orders, receipts and payments of services and things supplied to the organization and by the organization; records of orders and receipts of services and things made by one division of the organization upon other divisions of the same organization; and records, or better, accounts showing the condition of the organization with respect to funds appropriated to purchase services and things received and supplied, and amounts paid and due. Accounting also makes provision for giving summarized information periodically concerning the above data.

Our next step is to learn what documentary evidence superintendents and boards of education desire concerning their transactions; in what form accounts of transactions are kept; and finally, what information is required on the monthly summary or balance sheet.

A. Requisitions

There will first be examined certain documents required describing the various financial transactions of school systems. These documents include requisitions, orders, payrolls, and vouchers.

Every transaction within an organization originates in the need in some division for supplies or services. The officer or division whose duty it is to see to the supplying of that need is notified to do so by the receipt of requisitions from the division needing the services or things. We shall consider the various forms of requisitions in use in school administration.

TABLE XXII

A Summary of the Data Contained and Required on the Requisition Forms in Use in Sixteen Cities

ORIGINAL

	Goods Requisitioned for Which There Are Separate Forms Printed	Number of Copies	Source	To What Office Sent	Date	Point of Delivery	Time of Delivery	Item Number	Requisition Number	Order Number	Supply Department Number	Quantity	Units	Article	Description	Contents Printed—Number of Items	Price	Amount	Total
Auburn......		2	Name of School	Supt.	✓		✓		✓						✓				
Beverly......			Name of School		✓				✓	✓					✓				
Binghamton..			Dept. of Education	Board of Contract and Supply	✓				✓						✓				
Everett......	Supplies Books Paints etc. Janitors Supplies		Name of School		✓	✓		✓				✓	✓		✓	81 20+			
Lynn........	Janitorial Supplies	3	Name of School	Supply Dept.	✓		✓				✓	✓			✓	55+	✓	✓	
Malden......	Blanks etc. Janitors' Supp. Misc. Supp.		Name of School		✓											22 46			

Description of Documents of Expenditure

City														
Melrose									✓		✓			
Montclair	Supplies	2	Name of School	✓		✓			✓					
Newton	Supplies Text-books		Name of School	✓				✓	✓		✓	125+		
Niagara Falls	Material Books		Dept. School	✓				✓	✓		✓			
Poughkeepsie			Name of School	✓		✓	✓		✓		✓	50		
Schenectady		2	Dept. of Education	✓	✓	✓		✓	✓		✓		✓	✓
Somerville			Bureau of Contract and Supply	✓						✓		115		
Stamford	Text-books Supplies		Supt's Office	✓					✓		✓	78+/68+		
Utica			Name of School	✓				✓			✓	126		
Yonkers	Supplies Janitors' Supp.		Name of School	✓					✓			43+/22		

City	Certified	Color of Original	Column for Checking	Account Charged	Division Charged	Name of Requisitioner	Approved By	Receipt Signed By	Receipt Dated	Date of Placing Order	Amount on Hand	Amount Ordered	Amount Received	Date of Receipt of Requisition	Estimated Cost	Contents Same as Original	Color	Received By	To What Office Sent	Contents Same as Original	Remarks	To What Office Sent	Color
Auburn	Prin.	White								✓						✓	Yellow						
Beverly						✓									✓								
Binghamton	Prin.					Prin.																	
Everett	Prin.	White	✓	✓	✓							✓	✓			✓ except for 4 items	Blue	✓	Supply Dept.	✓ except for 4 items	✓	Prin.	Pink
Lynn	Prin.										✓	✓											
Malden	Prin.	White	✓	✓	✓											✓	Blue						
Melrose										✓				✓									
Montclair	Teacher Prin. Business Mgr. Chairman Com.																						
Newton	Prin.					✓	Supt.				✓	✓	✓										
Niagara Falls	Prin.					Prin.	Supt.	Prin.	✓														
Poughkeepsie											✓	✓	✓			✓	Pink						
Schenectady	✓	White															. .						
Somerville																							
Stamford	Prin.						Supt.	Prin.	✓														
Utica	Prin.																						
Yonkers								✓															

Description of Documents of Expenditure

From seventeen cities were obtained requisition blanks such as were in use in the schools. From other cities none could be obtained because such forms were not used or the offices visited could not furnish them.

A summary of the data contained and required on the requisition forms examined is given in Table XXII.

From this summary we find that eight cities use one form of requisition for all purposes, while other cities use one form for books and another for supplies, while Everett has one form for supplies, one for books, one for janitors' supplies and one for printed forms and kindergarten material.

Nine of the cities have one or more forms containing a printed list of articles from which the objects desired are to be chosen.

Requisitions are made both yearly and when needed.

Responsibility for the requisition is placed upon the principal, who shows his certification to the statements made by placing his signature upon the forms.

But four cities require more than one copy to be made out. In such case the principal keeps the duplicate copy, sending the original to the supply department or purchasing agent.

Study of this table shows that certain information is generally desired when requisitions for articles come in to the central office. The requisition must show:

1. Whence it comes.
2. The date when it is made out.
3. The quantity of goods desired.
4. The description of goods desired.
5. The signature of the principal, who thereby certifies that it is his opinion that the goods as listed and described are such as should be furnished the school.

The other information that may be contained in a requisition is shown in the variations in practice exhibited in Table XXII. However, there are data that should be contained in each requisition such as:

1. The names and sufficient description of the goods desired, to make their identification easy.
2. The name of the school from which the request comes.
3. The name of the grade from which the request comes.
4. The signature of the teacher making the request.

62   *School Costs and School Accounting*

Other data will be entered as is deemed necessary. Various requisitions in use are shown in the accompanying illustration.

Requisition in Use in Niagara Falls, N. Y.

* Original—To be Sent to the Secretary (white)

* Duplicate—To be Sent to the Secretary (blue)

* Triplicate—To be Retained by Principal (pink)
* Each is signed by Principal

Requisition in Use in Lynn, Mass.

Form 26,

MALDEN PUBLIC SCHOOLS.

REQUISITION FOR MISCELLANEOUS SUPPLIES.

.................................., 190

..............................SCHOOL

To the Superintendent of Schools:—
I beg to submit below a careful inventory of the stock of miscellaneous supplies now on hand at this building, together with an estimate of the additional quantities which will be required to supply all needs until..........................190

....

Principal.

	On Hand	Needed
1. Bells..........		
2. Blotters, for pupils (100's)................		
3. Blotters, for teachers' desks.............		
4. Calling Cards................		
5. Card-board, 22x28............		
6. Cardboard, 11x14..........		
7. Colored Sticks............		
8. Crayon, colored (boxes)..........		
9. Crayon, white (boxes)........		
10. Dennison's Fasteners, ½ inch..........		
11. Dennison's Fasteners, ¾ inch.........		
12. Erasers, blackboard (dozens).........		
13. Flags.............		
14. Ink, powder............		
15. Ink, red..........		
16. Ink Fillers............		
17. Ink Stands............		
18. Ink-wells, Chandler.........		
19. Ink-wells, Jacobus...........		
20. Ink-wells, Star..........		
21. Ink-well Covers...........		
22. Machine Oil...........		
23. Mucilage (quarts)..........		
24. Mucilage (bottles).........		
25. Pencils, gross...........		
26. Pencils, blue for teachers...........		
27. Pencil Sharpeners.............		
28. Pens (lower grades)...........		
29. Pens (higher grades)..........		
30. Penholders (gross)...........		
31. Pitchpipes............		
32. Pointers...........		
33. Rakes, blackboard..........		
34. Rubber Bands...........		
35. Rulers, 1 inch...........		
36. Rulers, ¼ inch...........		
37. Rulers, 1-16 inch...........		
38. Rulers, brass edge.........		
39. Sandpaper disks (dozens)..........		
40. Scissors............		
41. Thermometers............		
42. Twine, heavy............		
43. Twine, medium............		
44. Waste Baskets............		
45. Wooden Stools............		
46. Yard Sticks............		

N. B. Order by units unless otherwise indicated.
Let the number ordered be a multiple of 5 as far as possible.
Send one copy only of this requisition.

Requisition in Use in Malden, Mass.

But one city* was found that made use of a special printed form of request for services to be performed for repairs of equipment or buildings.

The form used is as follows:

REPAIRS

....190

To Committee on School Houses:—
  The following matters need attention at this building:

....Principal
....School

Ordered done..190
        by..
Completed.. 190
        Signed..

B. Purchase Orders

After many requisitions have been filled the supply of goods in the storeroom runs low and needs replenishing. Also there are demands for services and other supplies than those contained in the storeroom. These must be purchased from outside the organization. The order for goods is sent to the vendor on some standard form developed by the city as best serving its purpose. The forms of orders used in eleven cities are described in Table XXIII. Here we have much less variation in practice than was the case with requisitions. Of the eleven cities from which order forms were obtained we find that more than half of them

1. Make at least one copy of the order in addition to the original copy.
2. Necessarily enter the name of the vendor.
3. Give each order a serial number.
4. Enter the date of giving the order.
5. Necessarily describe the goods ordered.
6. Enter the price as obtained from some quotation or previous transaction.

*Requisition in Use in Everett, Mass.

Description of Documents of Expenditure 65

TABLE XXIII—SUMMARY OF THE DATA CONTAINED AND REQUIRED ON THE ORDER FORMS IN USE IN ELEVEN CITIES

	Number of Copies	Vendor	Date Paid	Route of Shipment	Date of Shipment	Order Number	Date of Order	Destination of Shipment	Quantity	Service	Description	Supplies	Price	Total of Extension	Endorsed by	Requisition Number	Fund to be Charged	Name of School	Unit Price	Item Number	Units	Date of Settlement of Accounts	Date of Presenting Bills	Estimated Cost	Color of Original	As to Prepayment of Shipment	Conveyance (ship goods by ...)	Terms	Approved by
Auburn	2	✓				✓	✓		✓		✓		✓		Supt.	✓		✓											
Beverly	3	✓				✓	✓		✓	✓	✓	✓	✓		Supt.		✓													
Binghamton	2	✓				✓	✓								Commissioner															
Elmira	2	✓				✓	✓				✓		✓		Sec.															
Lynn	3	✓		✓	✓	✓	✓								✓	✓														✓ Com.
Melrose	2	✓		✓		✓	✓								Supt.	✓														
Montclair	2	✓		✓	✓	✓	✓								Business Manager	✓														
Newton																														
Niagara Falls																														
Schenectady																														
Stamford																														

TABLE XXIII—Concluded

	Duplicate			Triplicate			Quadruplicate		
	Disposition	Contents Same	Color	Disposition	Contents Same	Color	Received in Good Condition	Contents Same	Color	Disposition
Auburn	Filed	✓	Yellow							
Beverly	Filed	✓	White	To prin. to be returned for checking	✓ except for directions	White				
Binghamton	Filed	✓ except no endorsement	Blue							
Elmira	Filed	✓	White							
Lynn	Filed	✓ except no directions	Blue	To Supply Dept. to check goods to be returned	✓ except no directions	Yellow	✓			
Melrose	Filed	✓	Yellow							
Montclair	Store Room	✓	Yellow							
Newton	Filed	✓	Yellow	To prin. for checking goods	No printed contents. Only entries in carbon	Blue	✓			
Niagara Falls	Sent to Vendor	✓	Yellow	Kept by Vendor	✓	Pink				
Schenectady	Filed in Compt's off.	✓	Blue	To Dept. of Educ. for checking	✓	Yellow		✓	Pink	Sent to Controller
Stamford										

7. Have the order endorsed by some officer representing the school board.

8. Enter the number of the requisition for which the order is given.

9. Have the duplicate copy of the order printed on different colored paper from that of the original.

10. File the duplicate copy for use in checking the goods received.

There is little change to be suggested in the data entered on an order. The variations in practice are shown in the illustrations.

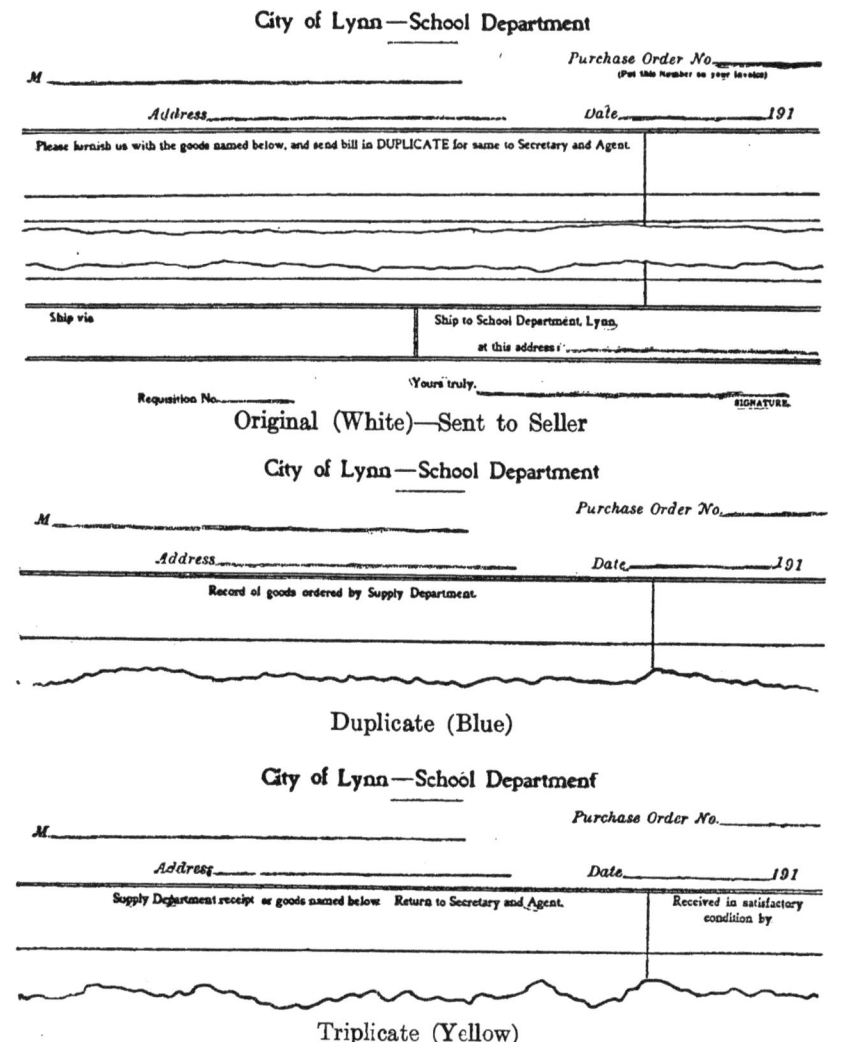

Original (White)—Sent to Seller

Duplicate (Blue)

Triplicate (Yellow)
To be Retained by the Supply Department Until Goods are Received
Purchase Order in Use in Lynn, Mass.

[Purchase Order form image]

Purchase Order in Use in Newton, Mass.

C. PAYROLLS

Table XXIV shows that of the more than seventy-three entries provided on the payrolls used in the eighteen cities listed, only four items are entered by ten or more of them. These items are:

1. The name of the school.
2. The name of the month.
3. The name of the payee.
4. The amount due.

There is no uniformity in the data required in the original document that describes the transactions between the school board and its employees whereby the board pays for personal services rendered it. A payroll should contain the following information:

1. The name of the payee.
2. The amount due the payee.
3. The time during which the payee rendered service.
4. The kind of service rendered.
5. The division of the school system that receives the service.

Other data can of course be entered, of which examples are given in the illustrations.

PAY ROLL
BOARD OF EDUCATION
POUGHKEEPSIE, N. Y,

_____ 191

NAME	POSITION	Regular Salary	Salary for Month	Reduction for Absence	Reduction for T. R. Fund	Amount Due

Face

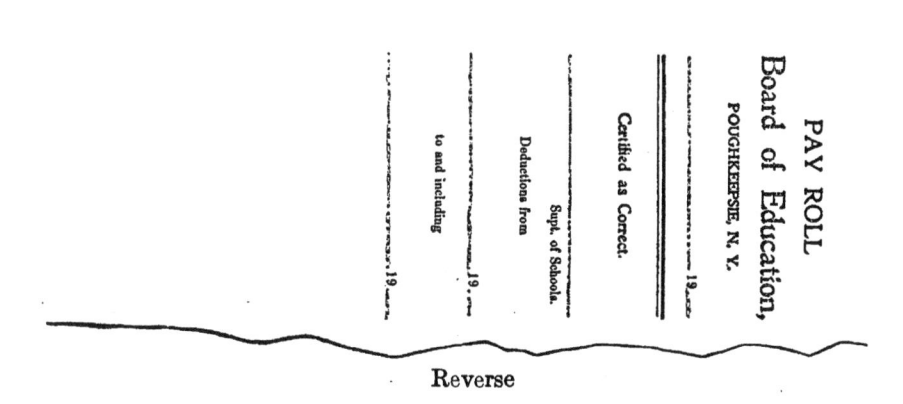

Reverse — PAY ROLL, Board of Education, POUGHKEEPSIE, N. Y. — Certified as Correct _____ 19___ — Supt. of Schools. — Deductions from _____ 19___ to and including _____ 19___

Payroll in Use in Poughkeepsie, N. Y.

School Costs and School Accounting

		NAME OF SUBST'T
Auburn (Time Report)	Prin.	✓ ✓ ✓ ✓ ✓ ✓ ✓ ✓ ✓
Beverly		✓ {✓ ✓} ✓ ✓ ✓ ✓ ✓ ✓ ✓ ✓
Binghamton	Prin. Clerk	✓ ✓ ✓ ✓ ✓ ✓ ✓ ✓ ✓ ✓ ✓ ✓ ✓ ✓ ✓ ✓
Chelsea		✓
Elmira		✓ ✓ ✓
Everett		✓ ✓
Hoboken	Supt.	✓
Lynn		✓
Malden		✓ ✓ ✓ ✓ ✓ ✓
Melrose		✓ ✓ ✓ ✓ ✓ ✓
New Rochelle	Clerk Pres.	✓ ✓ ✓ ✓
Newton		✓
Niagara Falls (Payroll and Time Report)	Prin. Pres. Clerk	✓ ✓ ✓ ✓ ✓
Orange	Pres. Supt.	✓ ✓ ✓
Port Chester		✓
Poughkeepsie		✓
Somerville (Payroll and Time Report)	Prin.	✓ ✓ ✓ ✓ ✓ ✓ ✓ ✓
Utica	Prin.	✓ ✓ ✓ ✓ ✓

																									Number of Rant
Auburn (Time Report)	✓			✓				✓	✓	✓										✓	✓				
Beverly			✓						✓		Finance Com.	Supt.			✓				Month						
Binghamton																✓								✓	
Chelsea																									
Elmira							✓							✓										✓	
Everett							✓								✓		Auditor		Month						
Hoboken			✓						✓																
Lynn																			Week						
Malden							✓												Month						
Melrose																									
New Rochelle							✓									✓	Con-troller Clerk	✓						✓	
Newton							✓		✓				✓	✓	✓				Month						
Niagara Falls (Payroll and Time Report)			✓		✓		✓												Month						
Orange					✓	✓																		✓	✓
Port Chester											Supt.								Month						
Poughkeepsie																✓									
Somerville (Payroll and Time Report)	✓				✓				✓											✓	✓	✓	✓		
Utica																									

School	Date	Receipt of Pay-Roll Noted	Date of Receipt	Date of Delivery of Check	Receipt of Payroll Signature Noting	Order Number	Check Number	Amount	Expense Ledger Folio	Fund Charged	Date of Audit	Date of Approval	Certified By	Approved By	Audited	Voucher Number	Check Counter-signed	Ordered Paid	Date Ordered Paid	Signed By	Check on—Bank
Auburn (Time Report)	✓																				
Beverly																					
Binghamton	✓												Supt. Chairman Finance								
Chelsea																					
Elmira																					
Everett																					
Hoboken	✓							✓	✓				Com. Finance					✓	✓	Pres. Sec.	
Lynn																					
Malden																					
Melrose																					
New Rochelle	✓	✓				✓	✓	✓				✓				✓	✓	✓			✓
Newton		✓				✓		✓								✓					
Niagara Falls (Payroll and Time Report)	✓		✓	✓	✓					✓	✓		Supt.	Teacher Com.	Finance Com.						
Orange																					
Port Chester	✓												Supt.								
Poughkeepsie																					
Somerville (Payroll and Time Report)	✓													Chairman Finance Com.	Clerk	✓					
Utica	✓																				

D. Vouchers

After goods have been received or services have been rendered the school system is under obligation to make payment of money for the same. The services or things purchased are described in a bill which is rendered to the school board. Before payment is made the school authorities must examine the bill to ascertain the validity of the charges in order that they may vouch for it and approve its payment. For this purpose bills are usually rendered or copied on a form supplied by the school board; on the reverse of the bill is a form to be filled out by the employees and representatives of the board vouching for the validity of the bill and the propriety of its payment, which form when filled may become an order on the proper officer to pay for the services and things supplied.

The entries contained in the vouchers in use in ten cities are described in Table XXV. In the data entered in these documents the majority of cities agree as to the important matters. Thus we find that most of them provide for making the following entries in the vouchers:

1. The date on which the statement is drawn up.
2. The name of the vendor.
3. The description of the services and things purchased.
4. The amount due on each item.
5. The total amount due.

On the reverse side:

6. The voucher number.
7. The amount vouched for.
8. The class of services or things purchased.
9. The name of the vendor.
10. The endorsement of the proper officers.

A voucher containing such entries would be satisfactory provided it contained also the date of the purchase, the number of the order on which it was made and the name of the appropriation to which the expenditure is to be charged. Forms of vouchers in use are shown in the illustrations.

THE CITY OF YONKERS
DEPARTMENT OF EDUCATION.

To _____ Dr.

ORDER MUST BE ATTACHED HERETO   Address _____

191	ORDER NO.	SCHOOL	ITEMS	PRICE	AMOUNT
			TOTAL		

NOTICE.—*The number of each order issued for this account must be inserted in the "Order No." column above, and on the same line with its item, and also the orders proper must accompany the bill, otherwise payment will not be made.*

I hereby Certify, That the merchandise, materials or articles enumerated in the above account have been received, and the services specified performed; that they were necessary for, and have been, or will be applied to the use of this Department, and I further certify, that no part of said account has been paid or satisfied.

Yonkers, _____ 191 ___   Signed _____

Title of office _____

Face

Claim No. _____ Warrant No. _____ Audited for $ _____ CLAIMANT FOR Account Charge to Bureau of WARRANT DRAWN Date APPROVED Comptroller. Warrant No. _____ within claim in settlement of Received for Audit—

Am't Claimed $ _____

READ THIS AFFIDAVIT

STATE OF NEW YORK,
COUNTY OF WESTCHESTER, } ss: _____ being duly sworn, says
CITY OF YONKERS,

*That deponent is duly authorized by claimant to make this affidavit and is fully acquainted with the facts herein stated, That the labor or services, merchandise, materials or articles charged in the within account or claim in the amount therein specified have been actually performed, made or delivered FOR THE CITY OF YONKERS; THAT THE ITEMS AND SPECIFICATIONS THEREIN ARE CORRECT; THAT THE SUMS CHARGED THEREFOR ARE REASONABLE AND JUST; and that no set-off exists, nor payment has been made on account thereof or claim assigned to other parties except such as are included or referred to in such account, and that claimant is not an employee of the City of Yonkers.

Subscribed and sworn to before me this _____
_____ day of _____ 191 ___   Signature of Person making the affidavit.

*Erase if made by claimant.
Sign your name very plainly and in full.

Reverse

Voucher in Use in Yonkers, N. Y.

Description of Documents of Expenditure 75

TABLE XXV.—A Summary of the Data Contained and Required on the Vouchers in Use in Ten Cities

	Date	Vendor	Place of Delivery	Date of Purchase	Description	Date of Delivery	To Whom Delivered	Quantity	Amount	Units	Price	Total	Item Number	Name of City	Date of Order	Affidavit	Order Number	School	Fund Charged	Requisition Number	Ordered By	Account	Number of Copies
Auburn	✓	✓		✓	✓				✓			✓		✓									1
Binghamton	✓				✓				✓			✓		✓	✓	✓	✓		✓	✓		✓	1
Elmira	✓	✓		✓	✓				✓					✓									1
Little Falls	✓	✓		✓	✓				✓			✓		✓									1
Niagara Falls	✓	✓		✓	✓				✓			✓		✓		✓							1
Poughkeepsie	✓	✓		✓	✓				✓			✓		✓									1
Schenectady		✓	✓		✓	✓	✓	✓	✓	✓	✓	✓	✓	✓			✓						5
Stamford																							1
Utica	✓	✓			✓				✓			✓		✓							✓		1
Yonkers	✓	✓			✓				✓		✓	✓		✓			✓	✓					1

TABLE XXV—Concluded (Reverse)

City	Treasurer's Voucher	Board of Education	Voucher Number	Amount	Check Number	Name of Bank	Check	Name of Bank	Name of Goods Purchased	Vendor	Date of Purchase	Account Charged	Fund Charged	Date of Audit	Amount	Number of Warrant	Distribution of Accounts	Endorsed By	Date of Warrant	Affidavit	Date of Receipt for Audit	Fiscal Year 19—	Claim Number	Errors	Amount Paid
Auburn		✓	✓	✓	✓	✓			✓	✓		✓	✓					—Com. Finance Com. Sec., Comr., Mayor, Clerk, Compt.				✓	✓	✓	✓
Binghamton		✓	✓	✓					✓		✓						✓								
Elmira	✓	✓	✓	✓	✓	✓	✓	✓	✓	✓	✓		✓	✓	✓			Pres. Clerk							
Little Falls			✓	✓					✓	✓			✓	✓	✓			—Com. Finance Com.							
Niagara Falls			✓	✓					✓	✓			✓			✓									
Poughkeepsie		✓	✓	✓														Com'r and Finance Com.							
Schenectady		✓	✓	✓						✓	✓	✓						Supt.—Com. Sec.							
Stamford			✓	✓					✓	✓					✓	✓	✓	Chairman Finance Com. Clerk Dep. Compt.							
Utica			✓	✓					✓	✓					✓	✓	✓	Compt.			✓				
Yonkers																			✓	✓	✓				

CHAPTER XI

DESCRIPTION AND USE OF VARIOUS LEDGERS

Our next problem is this: How do these cities bring together the data contained in original documents recording transactions and relate them to resources in order to learn their financial condition? Expenditures are made from certain funds; how are these expenditures related to such funds so as to show their condition? These questions can be answered only by studying methods in use in certain chosen cities that are examples of the practice in others.

In Amsterdam there was shown to the writer one book in which the accounts were kept. There were some thirteen columns, one for each of the following: Date, To Whom Paid, Number of Warrant, Amount, Teacher's Wages, High School, Repairs, Furniture, etc., Library, Contingent, Bonds and Interest, Regents, Coal. For each expenditure there were thus entered the date, the payee, the number of the warrant authorizing payment, the amount and the distribution of the amount to one or more of nine objects. This method accounts only for expenditures, does not distinguish between capital outlay and current expenditures, gives only some indefinite information concerning expenditures for kinds of schools, makes it impossible to learn the amount expended for administration, supervision, etc., and does not show the amounts spent for personal service, supplies, and other objects. Such accounting serves only to prove the faithfulness of the authorities charged with the expenditure of school funds.

In Port Chester expenditures were entered in a day book and posted from there to a ledger, which had an account for each appropriation, as credit against such appropriation. Each expenditure entered, together with information concerning it, was charged to some object of expenditure or other subject concerning which information was desired. This of course is the basis of all accounting. Other cities differ from Port Chester only in the way in which this is done. As used, Port Chester's method of accounting gives little of the information desired.

78   School Costs and School Accounting

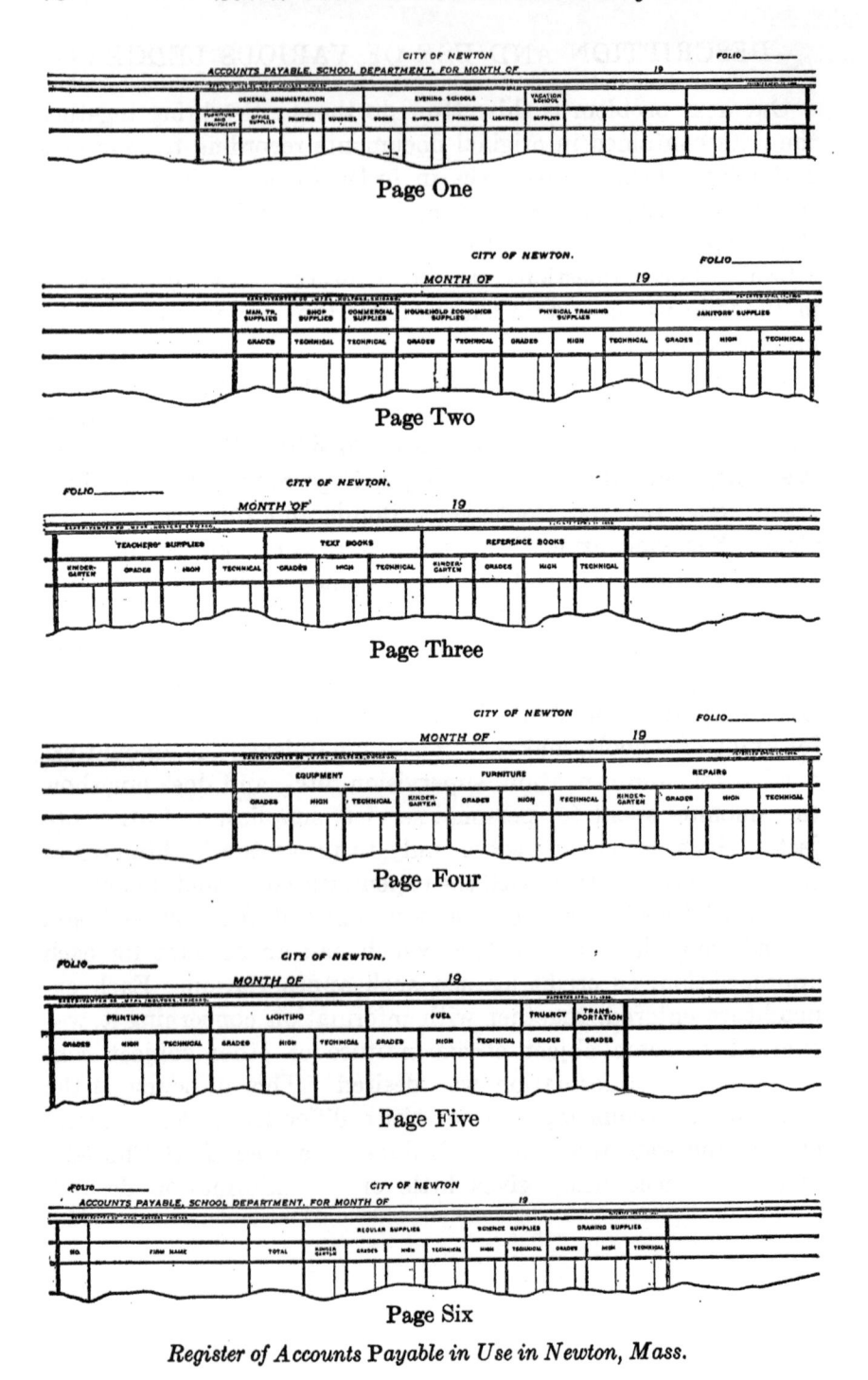

Page One

Page Two

Page Three

Page Four

Page Five

Page Six

Register of Accounts Payable in Use in Newton, Mass.

By having ledger accounts for each school this city would be able to provide very much of the information desired. The same is true of a majority of the cities visited and the accounting methods in use. They could be made efficient instruments in administration if the administrative officers felt a desire so to use them.

Newton makes use of the sheets shown in the illustration. Here are listed all bills to be paid. The objects to which the expenditures may be charged are sixty-two in number, each heading a column, in addition to which there are a column for the total expended and three blank columns. The number of the bill, the name of the vendor and the amount are entered in their proper columns, from which the total expended is distributed to the various objects. But even in Newton, where the superintendent of schools, Mr. Spaulding, has made more use of cost data in his work of administration than any school official met in the investigation, it is not possible to distinguish current expenditures from expenditures for capital outlay. And on these sheets on which it was stated that the "only record is made" there is no provision for entering expenditures for personal service for administration, supervision, instruction, and operation. Nor is there provision made for getting the amounts spent for supplies and other things used in supervision.

Of all the cities visited Lynn had provided the accounting system best adapted to accomplish the purposes that school accounting should serve. On the loose leaf sheets headed "Controlling Record of ACCOUNTS PAYABLE" there is entered the information as shown in the illustration. On the back of the

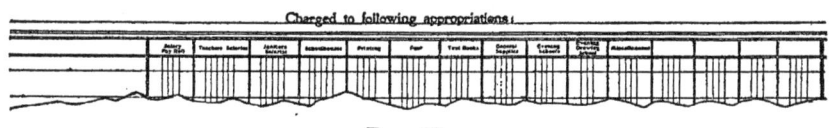

Page One

Page Two

Controlling Record of Accounts Payable in Use in Lynn, Mass.

following sheet, which, when bound is opposite the record of accounts payable, are columns headed by the titles of appropriations in which columns expenditures are entered and thereby charged to the proper appropriations. On the record of accounts payable there is a column in which are indicated for what division of the school organization the expenditure is made and the object for which the expenditure is made. This shows the division of the organization, for each of which there is in the ledger a separate sheet or group of sheets on which there is a column for each of the objects to which expenditures are charged. In the case of repairs and alterations, instead of a column there is provided for each school a sheet on which is given the desired information concerning each transaction.

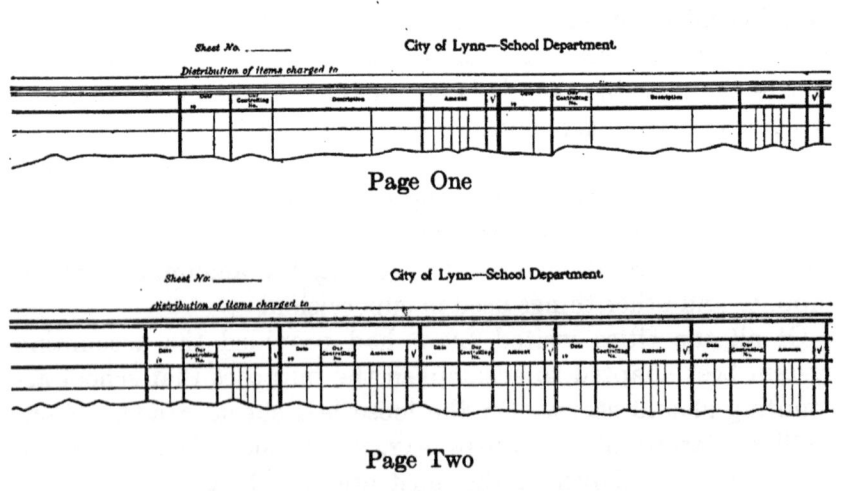

Page One

Page Two

School Ledger Sheet in Use in Lynn, Mass.

From this city there was obtained more accurate information than from any other, yet even here we cannot get true costs nor accurate expenditures for each kind of school—because expenditures for cooking are not distributed and evening schools do not receive their share of expenditures and because various expenditures for such objects as drawing supplies, graduation expense, and special teachers' salaries are not distributed; nor can there be obtained information concerning each character of expenditure or each object of expenditure.

Page One

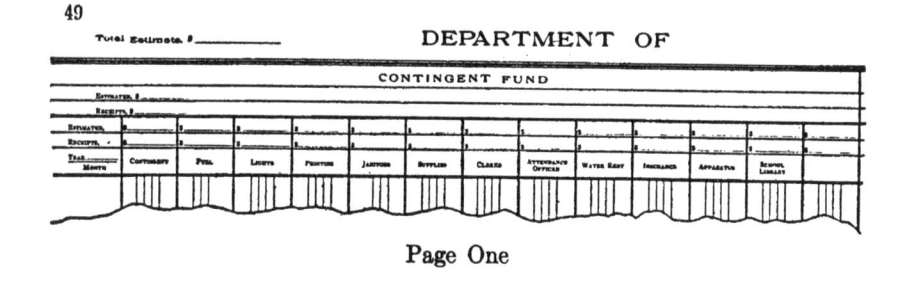

Page Two
Ledger in Use in Niagara Falls, N. Y.

The above has had to do with the means used in bringing together data concerning transactions so as to show the condition of school funds that must meet the obligations incurred in such transactions. These transactions have all been those to which the school system is a party. There are other transactions that take place within a school system itself. Certain of these we have mentioned, such as the requisitioning for supplies. One division of the school organization asks another division of the same organization to furnish it with certain articles of supplies. The requisition blank endorsed corresponds with the purchasing order sent from the school organization to an outside party. In the former case, data concerning transactions were brought together to get information concerning the condition of funds of school money. Here data concerning transactions are brought together to learn the condition of funds of school supplies which have been accepted as the exact equivalent of certain amounts of school moneys. Thus another problem is to learn what account is kept of school supplies.

But three cities were found that kept a continuous record of supplies. These were Lynn, Montclair, and Schenectady. Many other cities take inventory once a year, while New Haven was found to do so twice a year. Some cities apparently had no record of supplies once they were issued to the schools. In these cities the various divisions of the school organization receive supplies that were the equivalent of money and apparently no further questions are asked. Lynn, Montclair, and Schenectady have a continuous record of supplies on hand and of the divisions receiving such supplies, to which divisions charges may be made for the supplies that they receive.

Stock Book in Use in Lynn, Mass.

Montclair keeps a stock record card of each article of supplies and the unit used in carrying on transactions in it. On the card are also spaces, one for the minimum quantity of stock permitted to be on hand, the other to indicate the maximum to be ordered. When the quantity on hand reaches the minimum, a purchasing order must be issued for the quantity indicated as the maximum. A similar record is kept of books used except that no minimum or maximum quantities are entered on the cards.

Book Record Card in Use in Montclair, N. J.

Lynn made use of a sheet like that shown in the illustration for each article of supplies. A card was also used for wood and another for coal for each school. These cards were open to inspection by the janitors and were being used for the third year when the city was visited. It was stated that each year since their introduction the unit cost for fuel had decreased over that of the preceding year. The sheet and cards used by Lynn supply

Description of Various Ledgers 83

Face

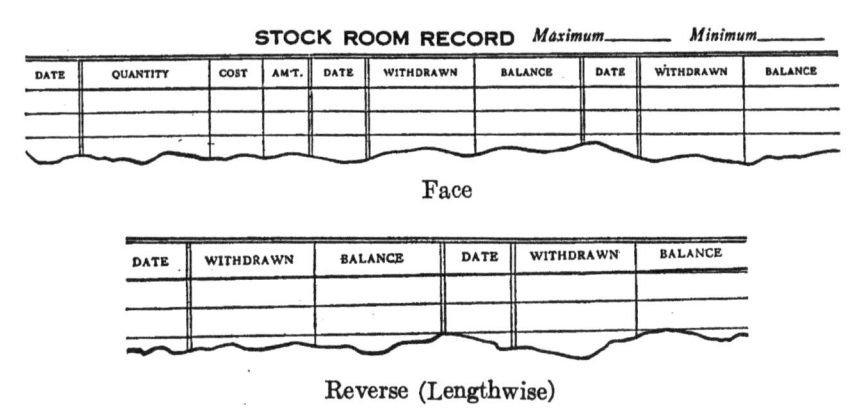

Reverse (Lengthwise)

Stock Room Record Card in Use in Schenectady, N. Y.

Coal Record Card in Use in Lynn, Mass.

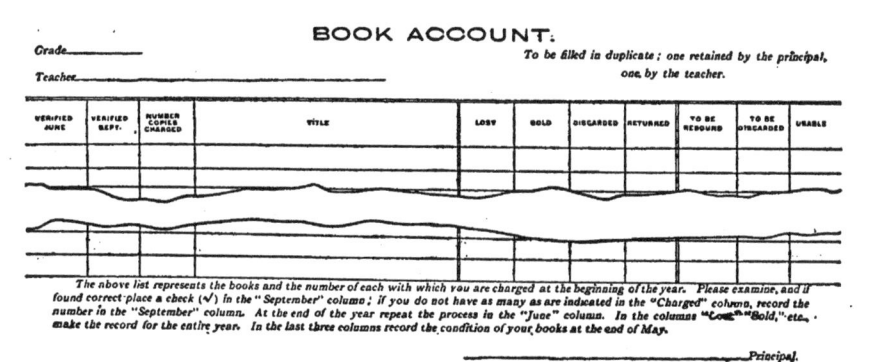

Book Account in Use in Everett, Mass.

the same information as those used by Montclair. The information contained on the card used by Schenectady is shown in the illustration. Each of these cities is able to tell at any time the value and quantity of supplies on hand in the storeroom and the quantity issued to any school or all schools. Lynn and Montclair are able to learn whether one school is using more than its share of goods. However, the schools are charged for the goods issued to them, but not the division of the schools using the goods. Because of this defect it is not possible to learn the cost of supplies used in teaching any grade in the elementary school or any subject in the high school.

We have found that the boards of education of all school systems account currently for the funds entrusted to them; the boards of education of three cities account currently for the sup-

Text-book Record Card — Primary Grades

_____ School _____ Principal _____ Date

TITLE	PUB.	GRADE	FIT FOR USE	NEED'D	TITLE	PUB.	GRADE	FIT FOR USE	NEED'D
Aesop's Fables	G.				Cyr's Primer	G.			
All the Year Round, Autumn	G.				Cyr's, I	G.			
All the Year Round, Winter	G.				Cyr's II	G.			
All the Year Round, Spring	G.				Cyr's III	G.			
All the Year Round, Summer	G.								
Andersen's Fairy Tales, I	G.				First Nature Reader	A.B.C.			
Arnold Primer	S. B.								
					Graded Literature, I	M. M.			
Baldwin's, I	A.B.C.				Graded Literature, II	M. M.			
Baldwin's, II	A.B.C.				Graded Literature, III	M. M.			
Baldwin's III	A.B.C.				Grimm's Fairy Tales	G.			
Baldwin's Fairy Tales and Fables	A.B.C.								
					Hawthorne, I	Globe			
Carroll's Around the World, I	S. B.				Hawthorne II	Globe			
Child Life in Many Lands	R. M.				Hawthorne, III	Globe			
Child Life Primer	Mac.				Hiawatha Primer	H. M.			
Child Life, I	Mac.								
Child Life, II	Mac.				In Mythland, I	Educ.			
Child Life III	Mac.				In Mythland, II	Educ.			

Face

TITLE	PUB.	GRADE	FIT FOR USE	NEED'D	TITLE	PUB.	GRADE	FIT FOR USE	NEED'D
Jones, I	G.				Ward's Primer	S. B.			
Jones, II	G.				Ward's I	S. B.			
Jones III	G.				Ward's, II	S. B.			
					Ward's III	S. B.			
Morse Copy Book, I	S. B.	1							
Morse Copy Book, II	S. B.	2							
Morse Copy Book, III	S. B.	3							
Nature's Byways	S. B.								
Nichol's Arithmetic, II	T. B.								
Normal First Music Reader	S. B.								
Scudder's Fables and Folk Stories	H. M.								
Stepping Stones, I	S. B.								
Stepping Stones, II	S. B.								
Stepping Stones, III	S. B.								
Stories of Great Americans for Little Americans	A.B.C.								
Stories of Great Men	Educ.								
Sunbonnet Babies' Primer	R. M.								
Tymer's Stories for Young Children	G.								

Reverse

Text-book Record Card in Use in Malden, Mass.

plies purchased by them; but not one city was found in which the board of education accounted currently for the property entrusted to it and purchased by it. In no city was there found any ledger or other means by which were recorded and related all the transactions that took place between the school organization or any division of it and any of its property. The school board of each city received for its disbursement during the year certain funds, of the expenditure of which it kept accurate record. At the beginning of the year it likewise received for its administration certain property. Of the value of that property at the beginning of the year it had no record; of the worth of the property at the end of the year it furnished no record. It rendered no full accounting of the decrease in value of the property due to depreciation and other causes; and of the increase in value of the property due to alterations and additional equipment it rendered no accounting;—though the value of the property entrusted to each board of education was worth many times the appropriations of money entrusted to it.

CHAPTER XII

DESCRIPTION AND USE OF FINANCIAL STATEMENTS

The last problem is to learn in what form periodical, preferably monthly, statements are rendered to enable the public, if it desires, and especially the legislative body, the board of education, to have such information as will give them a true and complete knowledge of the financial condition of the school system.

For the board of education of Auburn there are rendered two monthly statements, a financial statement, and a schedule of expenditures. As shown in the illustration, in the monthly financial statement are given the receipts from various sources, under disbursements the expenditures for certain large appropriation items, under balances the amounts on deposit in various banks and the amount of cash. A "Special Building Account" is reported upon in addition to the above. The disbursements under the large items of appropriations are further analyzed in a second statement as shown in the illustration.

The financial statement makes possible the comparison of one month with another; but it does not permit comparison of one month with the corresponding month of a previous year nor does it show the total expended to date. The accounts listed in the second statement have the defects mentioned previously in our study of costs. The statement enables one to make a comparison from month to month simply of expenditures for certain objects; it gives no statement of expenditures in terms of services performed.

The city of Beverly presents a statement that is more useful though peculiar in certain respects. Three columns make possible the comparison of the expenditures for the period this year with the corresponding period of two previous years. The statement gives, in addition to expenditures and the total expended, the amount of obligations contracted in the form of salaries to be paid, for maintenance, for bills on hand, and for fixed charges for the remainder of the year. The sum of the total amounts expended and contracted, deducted from the total of

Description of Financial Statements

BOARD OF EDUCATION. Monthly Financial Statement.

General Account.
Receipts.
Balance, Aug. 1,
City taxes,
State Apportionments,
Tuition,
Interest,
Miscellaneous,
    Total.

Disbursements.
Deficit, Aug. 1,
Salaries,
Supplies and expenses,
Equipments,
Buildings and sites,
    Total.

Balances.
Nat. Bank of Auburn,
Cayuga Co. Nat. Bank,
E. R. Fay & Sons,
Wm. H. Seward & Co.,
Cash,
    Total.

Special Building Account.
Receipts.

    Total.

Disbursements.

    Total.

Balances.
Nat. Bank of Auburn,
Cayuga Co. Nat. Bank,
E. R. Fay & Sons,
Wm. H. Seward & Co.
Cash,
    Total.

Monthly Financial Statement in Use in Auburn, N. Y.

SCHEDULE ONE.

Salaries.
   Superintendent, Clerks, Officers.
   Teachers, Principals and Supervisors.
   Medical Inspectors,
   Janitors.
                                              Total.			

Supplies and Expenses.
   Administration Supplies and Expenses.
   Janitor Supplies and Expenses.
   Miscellaneous School Supplies and Expenses.
   Manual Training Supplies and Expenses.
   Domestic Science Supplies and Expenses.
   Pupils' Free Supplies.
   Text Books for Indigent Pupils.
   Fuel.
   Lights.
   Power.
   Water.
   Insurance.
   Printing.
   Lectures and Entertainments.
   Miscellaneous Expenses.
                                              Total.			

Equipments.
   Apparatus.
   Furniture and Furnishings.
   Pictures and Casts.
   Library.
                                             Total.			

Buildings and Sites.
   Repairs and Improvements.
   New Sites.
   New Buildings.
                                             Total.			

Monthly Financial Statement, Schedule One, in Use in Auburn, N. Y.

amounts received and available, gives the working balance for the remainder of the year; which makes this statement of real help to the school authorities. But one wonders why expenditures except for salaries are considered as for maintenance. The term maintenance is usually used to mean something very much different from "everything but salaries." The statement from Beverly is good as a presentation of the financial condition of the school system as regards its moneys. There is no statement giving an analysis of expenditures.

CITY OF BEVERLY   SCHOOL DEPARTMENT
Expenditures—Comparisons—Balances
DATED _____

	19	19	19
ADMINISTRATION SALARIES			
INSTRUCTORS' SALARIES			
JANITORS' SALARIES			
TOTAL SALARIES			
MAINTENANCE: BUILDINGS			
MAINTENANCE: SUPPLIES			
MAINTENANCE: MISCELLANEOUS			
TRANSPORTATION			
SUPPORT OF TRUANTS			
TOTAL MAINTENANCE			
TOTAL EXPENDED			
OBLIGATIONS CONTRACTED { 1 Salaries / 2 Maintenance / 3 Bills on hand }			
TOTAL EXPENDED AND CONTRACTED			
WORKING BALANCE { Salaries / Maintenance A }			
Total fixed charges for balance of year*			
Free for use on Maintenance: Buildings			
" " " " Maintenance: Supplies A			
" " " " Maintenance: Miscellaneous			
*See Detail.			

Monthly Statement of Expenditures in Use in Beverly, Mass.

Of the form and content of the financial statement of Little Falls we have no knowledge. Probably, as in Auburn, it is a simple statement of receipts, expenditures, and the balances to be expended. Little Falls does, however, distribute its expenditures each month in a "distribution book" in accordance with the form shown in the illustration which was taken from one of its pages. This distribution is defective as shown early in the study; also it permits no quick comparison of month with month of the same or previous years nor does it show the total expended to date nor even the balance to be expended with comparisons of these amounts with those of previous years. This form provides for but the first step toward a proper statement of expenditures.

CITY OF LITTLE FALLS, N. Y.

Department of Public Schools

Expenditure for Each School in the Month of................191....

Designation of Account	General Expense	High School	Benton Hall	Church Street	Jefferson Street	Library	Domestic Science	Manual Training
Teachers Regular............								
Substitute..........								
Music..............								
Drawing...........								
Physical Training...								
Kindergarten.......								
Domestic Science ...								
Elocution..........								
Manual Training....								
Total Teachers..........								
Libraries.................								
Free Text-books............								
School Apparatus...........								
Sites and Permanent Improvements.................								
Repairing School Houses.....								
Insurance.................								
Fences, Sidewalks, etc........								
Furniture.................								
Printing, Stationery and Office Exp's.................								
Fuel and Lighting...........								
Janitors and Janitors' Supplies								
Supplies.................								
Water Tax.................								
Bond and Interest...........								
Miscellaneous...............								
Superintendent..............								
Clerk.....................								
Librarian..................								
Attendance Officers..........								
Other Officers..............								
Total Contingent........								
Grand Total............								

Monthly Statement of Expenditures in Use in Little Falls, N.Y.

The monthly distribution of expenditures of Malden is subject to the same criticism as that of Auburn with the exception that Malden does show the expenditures for each division of the school system. Yet, because a separate sheet is made out for each school, it is difficult to compare quickly the schools one with another.

Monthly Financial Statement in Use in Malden, Mass.

In Lynn, the statement of expenditures is given as shown in the illustration. It is a financial statement, simply comparing expenditures to date for the objects listed with the amounts estimated for the year giving the balances unexpended and making comparison with the same period of the preceding year. There is no statement of expenditures for the various divisions of the school organization such as Lynn is able to give and such as would be most helpful to the school authorities.

EXPENDITURES FOR NINE MONTHS ENDING OCTOBER 1, 1912

	Estimated Expenditures for 1912	Expended to Oct. 1, 1912	Expended to Oct. 1, 1911	Balance of Appropriation Unexpended	Overdrawn
1. Salary Pay Roll.	$13,381.67	$9,921.22	$10,697.84	$3,460.45	
2. Day Teachers' Salaries.	279,625.30	189,388.00	189,562.38	90,237.30	
3. Janitors' Salaries.	29,709.00	21,581.61	20,466.44	8,127.39	
4. Evening Teachers' Salaries.	8,850.00	3,714.00	3,752.00	5,136.00	
5. Evening Janitors' Salaries.	1,238.75	514.50	467.00	724.25	
6. Pensions.	900.00	675.00	300.00	225.00	
7. Schoolhouse Repairs, Alterations, Rent, etc.	11,350.00	7,351.78	12,627.45	3,998.22	
8. Fuel.	15,500.00	13,552.82	11,860.02	1,947.18	
9. Printing.	1,000.00	903.39	1,235.10	96.61	
10. Text-books.	5,000.00	5,689.27	8,284.86		$689.27
11. Reference Books.			132.80		
12. Teachers' and Pupils' Supplies.	9,000.00	6,536.60	8,337.17	2,463.40	
13. Janitors' Supplies.	900.00	881.61	924.08	18.39	
14. Horse and Wagon Expense.	918.33	678.68	380.50	239.65	
15. Express and Delivery.	500.00	332.70	392.26	167.30	
16. Washing Towels and Belts.	440.00	256.92	296.64	183.08	
17. Light and Power.	2,700.00	2,280.90	1,759.60	419.10	
18. Telephones.	660.00	514.50	595.98	145.50	
19. E. H. S. Laboratory Service.			56.00		
20. Graduation Expense.	450.00	534.45	456.32		84.45
21. Commitment of Truants.	2,600.00	1,763.28	1,268.50	836.72	
22. Advertising.	60.00	37.15	24.95	22.85	
23. Transportation and Expense of Officers.	110.66	75.04	60.91	35.62	
24. Transportation of Children.	550.00	300.00	250.00	250.00	
25. Committee Expense.	17.00	5.00	10.45	12.00	
26. School Census.	685.50			685.50	
27. Tuition.	60.00	48.28	6.00	11.72	
	$386,206.21	$267,536.70	$274,205.25	$118,669.51	$773.72
Receipts to Oct. 1, 1912.	$715.75				
Receipts to Oct. 1, 1911.	892.04				

Monthly Statement of Expenditures, Lynn, Mass.

The city of Newton gives a statement for the year to date of appropriations, amounts expended and unexpended for regular schools and vocational schools providing for comparison with the previous year. These are further analyzed as shown in the illustration. This statement, surpassing that of Beverly in showing for what expenditures have been made, does not have the great advantage of the Beverly statement in showing the obligations contracted and the funds available.

NEWTON SCHOOL COMMITTEE

	REGULAR	VOCATIONAL	TOTAL
SALARIES			
Teachers			
Superintendent			
Secretary			
Clerks			
Truant Officer			
Janitors			
Total			
INCIDENTALS			
Books			
School Supplies			
Janitors' Supplies			
Repairs			
Furniture			
Printing			
Truancy			
Lighting			
Miscellaneous			
Total			
FUEL			
Wood			
Coal			
Gas			
Total			
CONVEYANCE OF PUPILS			
EVENING SCHOOLS			
Salaries — Teachers			
Salaries — Janitors			
Fuel			
Incidentals			
Total			
VACATION SCHOOLS			
Salaries — Teachers			
Salaries — Janitors			
Incidentals			
Total			
TECH. SCHOOL EQUIPMENT			
GRAND TOTAL			

Monthly Statement of Expenditures in Use in Newton, Mass.

REGULAR SCHOOLS

The Chairman presented the following report of appropriations, expenditures and unexpended balances for the current fiscal year: (   )

	APPROPRIATION	EXPENDED	UNEXPENDED
Salaries. 19			
Supplies and Incidentals. 19			
Fuel. 19			
Conveyance of Pupils. 19			
Evening Schools. 19			
Vacation Schools. 19			
Technical High Equipment 19			
Receipts from Tuition. 19			
Receipts from Dog Tax. 19			
School Income. 19			
Appropriation. 19			
Total, 19			
Total, 19			

Monthly Statement of Expenditures for Regular Schools in Use in Newton, Mass.

VOCATIONAL SCHOOLS

The Chairman presented the following report of appropriations, expenditures and unexpended balances for the current fiscal year: (   )

	APPROPRIATION	EXPENDED	UNEXPENDED
DAY			
Salaries.			
19			
Supplies and Incidentals.			
19			
Fuel.			
19			
EVENING			
19			
RECEIPTS FROM TUITION.			
Day			
19			
Evening			
19			
SCHOOL INCOME.			
Day			
19			
Evening			
19			
STATE REIMBURSEMENT.			
Day			
19			
Evening			
19			
GENERAL APPROPRIATION.			
19			
Total, 19			
Total, 19			

Monthly Statement of Expenditures for Vocational Schools in Use in Newton, Mass.

In Poughkeepsie Superintendent Shear, dissatisfied with the financial facts supplied to those in authority when he came to

MEMORANDUM—SEPTEMBER 4, 1912

	APPROPRIATIONS	DISBURSEMENTS	BALANCE	
General Expense	$5,378.09	$5,271.64	$106.45	
Clerk	500.00	400.00	100.00	
Carpenter	840.00	560.00	280.00	
Furniture	500.00	149.00	351.00	
Fuel and Light	4,700.00	4,843.28	000.00	−$143.28
Insurance	800.00	952.60	000.00	− 152.60
Janitors' Salaries	5,500.00	3,577.36	1,922.64	
Night School	1,000.00	667.00	333.00	
Printing	600.00	390.77	209.23	
Repairs	6,500.00	3,000.58	3,499.42	
Supplies	3,000.00	2,113.91	886.09	
Superintendent	3,000.00	2,000.00	1,000.00	
Text-books	3,000.00	2,519.11	480.89	
Compulsory Education	1,200.00	644.35	555.65	
Teachers' Salaries	71,000.00	40,931.85	30,068.15	
Teachers' Ret. Fund	3,968.85	1,050.00	2,918.85	
Playgrounds and V. S.	700.00	389.91	310.09	
School Nurse	700.00	390.00	310.00	
Upper Church St.	78,712.50	53,154.00	25,558.50	
	$191,599.44	$123,005.36	$68,889.96	−$295.88

NOTE.
High School 340.75

Total Disbursements $123,346.11

Monthly Statement of Expenditures, Poughkeepsie, N. Y.

DISBURSEMENTS BY SCHOOLS
of the City of Poughkeepsie, N. Y., for the month ended_____ 191_

	No. 1	No. 2	No. 3	No. 5	No. 6	No. 8	No. 9	No. 10	C.G.S.	P.H.S.	K.M.	H. for F.	Night Sch'l	Office	Total
Supervisors															
Teachers															
Janitors															
At'nd'ce Officer															
School Nurse															
School Carpenter															
Total Salaries															
Gen'l Expense															
Clerks															
Furniture															
Fuel and Light															
Insurance															
Printing															
Repairs															
Supplies															
Text-books															
Teachers' Retirement Fund															
Play Grounds & Va't'n Schools															

Monthly Statement of Expenditures in Use in Poughkeepsie, N. Y.

that city, determined to know what was being expended for each division of his system. The form shown in the illustration was introduced by him to gain this information. While it is possible to compare expenditures by schools as in Little Falls and other cities, yet as in those cities it is not possible to compare the expenditures for this month with the expenditures for any other period. The change in Poughkeepsie is an instance of the desire on the part of the administrative officer for financial data that will aid him in performing his function more efficiently than he could with financial data that show only the amounts received, expended, and on hand.

From the statements studied we find that

1. No city demands periodically a complete statement of revenue and expense.

2. No city renders any statement of the condition of the properties entrusted to it.

3. But one city, Beverly, states the amount of obligations already incurred at the date of rendering the statement which enables the school authorities to know the amount available for other purposes.

The preceding pages show the extent to which the inability of cities to furnish the data desired is due to the inadequate mechanism used by the school authorities in recording, treating and reporting financial facts. Helpful information can be recorded and become useful only after the forms and methods for its collection and treatment have been provided and elaborated. This problem is considered in Part Three.

PART III

A SYSTEM OF SCHOOL ACCOUNTING RECOMMENDED

CHAPTER XIII

PURPOSES TO BE SERVED BY THE ACCOUNTING SYSTEM RECOMMENDED

The following pages are given to the explanation of a system of accounting, the use of which shall enable school authorities to answer for themselves the questions that this investigation set out to answer. The methods used in this system include certain methods already described in the preceding pages, gathered in the visits to the cities listed, others obtained from investigation of accounting as carried on in manufacturing concerns of different types, and from material obtained from the "Manual of Accounting and Business Procedure for the City of New York," 1909, and the "Advance Sheets of Standard Departmental Forms for Accounting and Reporting" effective in Philadelphia on January 1, 1913.

Every step taken in the system of accounting here described is to accomplish one or more of these three purposes:

1. To provide for each transaction an original document that will contain a complete history of the transaction from its beginning to its completion, including the fixing of personal responsibility for each step taken, and will serve as the best evidence obtainable to protect the city in any action that might be taken as a result of the transaction.

2. To make it possible for those in authority to account for funds appropriated for school purposes.

3. To furnish the administrative officers such information as will enable them to decide whether every service is performed at the lowest cost compatible with maximum efficiency.

If the reader finds in this system of accounting that which he believes is unnecessary or requires too much labor or for some other reason is not suitable, he must apply each of these tests. If the step under consideration does not meet any of these tests the reader's judgment is correct. Otherwise it is not. There is nothing recommended here that has not been found in principle in use in public accounting of funds or in industrial accounting of costs. Steps that seem to require the greatest expenditure of time have been found in industry to be necessary to the greatest efficiency, which must be based on complete knowledge.

The system is such that it may be installed gradually or all at once. At first it may be desired to get costs by school buildings or it may be desired to go further and keep accurate records for each individual room. However, as finally installed and used, the writer believes that costs should be recorded at least by grades in each elementary school and by subjects in each high school. The system described has been designed to give costs thus, i.e., by grades in elementary schools and by subjects in high schools.

In a few school systems, especially those where the superintendent thinks that school finances are none of his affairs, the installation of such a system would mean an additional expenditure of $1800 for clerk and assistant. It is the confident belief of the writer, based on the knowledge of results in industry, that such accounting of school funds will save to a city many times more than is required for its operation.

The forms to be used are the following:

Forms Recommended

Requisition for Supplies.
Work Requisition.
Purchase Order.
Purchase Order Voucher.
Payroll for Elementary Schools.
Principal's Time Sheet.
Payroll for Supervisors and Special Teachers.
Time Sheets of Supervisors and Special Teachers.
Expense Ledger Sheet for Each Grade or Subject.
Expense Ledger Sheet for Each School.

Expense Ledger Sheet for General Administration.
Property Ledger Sheet.
Supply and Text-book Ledger Sheet.
Supply Tag.
Appropriation Ledger Sheet.
General Balance Sheet.
Monthly Statement of Supplies in Use.
Monthly Property Statement.
Monthly Statement of Expenditures.
Monthly *D*istribution of Expense.
Monthly Statement of Unit Costs for General Administration and for each School.
Monthly Statement of Unit Costs for each Grade.

CHAPTER XIV

DESCRIPTION AND USE OF EXPENDITURE DOCUMENTS RECOMMENDED

A. Requisitions

Most of the transactions in a school system have their beginning in some grade in which children are being taught. It takes the form of a lack of some article of supplies, or arises from the failure of some part of the equipment or structure that needs repairing, or from the need for some special service. In a small school the teacher will walk to the home of a school trustee and will ask him to see that the article or service is supplied; or she will write him to that effect. She wastes her time in doing either. A standard form makes necessary the smallest amount of writing. A requisition blank is such a form used to state a request for supplies or services. The requisition blank here used is made out in triplicate. It contains the following information on the original copy:

1. The requisition number is entered by the secretary and serves to identify the requisition and to give it a place in the serial order of requisitions received.

2. The numbers of the room and grade designate what subdivision of the school organization needs the goods or services, enable the secretary to examine his records to learn whether the requisition should be granted, and enable him also to make the charge for the goods or services directly to the subdivision of the system receiving them.

3. Likewise the name of the school identifies the destination of the goods or services and later makes it possible to get the total cost of the same supplied to each school.

4. The date on or before which delivery is desired is given to enable the person who delivers the goods to do so at his convenience, yet to insure their being on hand when desired.

5. The description given in the column headed "Description" identifies the goods or services for all persons having to do with

Requisition for Text-books and Supplies

the requisition. The three forms can be still further standardized by printing the names of the articles in their proper column. Such an arrangement would be most helpful at those stated times, as at the beginning of the year, when requisitions are made for many articles. The blank form here shown could then be used during the period when goods or services are desired only irregularly.

6. The amount given as the quantity in stock enables the principal and later the secretary to decide whether the request shall be granted. It enables the secretary also to check up the teacher's statement of amount on hand with the amount as shown by his own records. It should also result in the teacher's taking better care of the supplies furnished her.

7. The number requested must of course be given to show what quantity is desired.

8. In the fourth column the secretary will enter the quantity of each article that he orders the storekeeper to deliver to the person making the requisition.

9. In the next column the secretary will show, by a check opposite each article, that he has received the statement of the storekeeper containing the signature of the teacher showing that the goods have been received.

10. In the last column the secretary will also enter the cost of the quantity of each article delivered.

11. No requisition is honored unless it has the signature of the teacher desiring the goods.

12. The date shows when the requisition was originally made out.

13. The principal's signature shows his belief that the request should be granted.

14. The date shows the time when his approval was given.

15. The signature of the secretary is necessary to show that he has ordered the goods delivered as stated.

16. The date after the secretary's name shows at what time he gave his order for the goods to be delivered.

17. The date of delivery of goods is shown as taken from the statement of the storekeeper.

18. The second signature of the secretary shows his endorsement of the storekeeper's statement that the goods have been delivered.

19. The secretary's memorandum shows that he has made the proper entries on the supply and text-book record sheets reserving the quantities requisitioned and making the proper deductions in the quantities available.

20. The secretary's memorandum with date shows that he has entered on the supply and text-book record sheets the quantities delivered and the quantities remaining in stock.

21. The secretary's memorandum with date shows that he has charged on the ledger sheet for the proper division the stock delivered to it.

The duplicate and triplicate copies contain the following as on the original copy:

1. Requisition number.
2. Numbers of room and grade.
3. Name of school.
4. *D*esired date of delivery.
5. *D*escription of articles.
6. Quantity on hand.
7. Quantity requested.
8. Quantity ordered delivered.
9. Signature of teacher with date.
10. Signature of principal with date.
11. Signature of secretary with date.
12. Check to show that goods have been received.

The duplicate copy has in addition:

1. The signature of the teacher to show the goods have been received as checked.
2. The date on which the goods were received.
3. The signature of the person delivering the goods.
4. The date on which he delivered the goods.

The triplicate, in addition to the eleven entries listed, not including the secretary's signature and date of same, also provides for entering the date on which the goods were received in order that the principal may have it in his files.

The procedure in the use of the blanks is as follows:

The teacher, using two sheets of carbon paper, enters on the three copies the number of the grade, the name of the school, the latest date on which she wishes the goods delivered, the description of the articles desired, the quantity she has on hand, the quantity she desires, and signs her name with date showing when she makes out the requisition. The three copies are forwarded to the principal. The principal examines the requisition, and using two sheets of carbon signs the copies to show that he approves the requisition, giving the date of his approval. He keeps the triplicate copy on file. The original and duplicate copies are sent to the secretary, who should examine the requisition to see whether the quantity on hand warrants the issue of the goods, whether the quantity on hand is what it should be according to the ledger sheet of the grade. If, after examination, he believes the goods or any part of them should be delivered, the secretary enters in the column "Ordered Delivered" the quantity of each article that he will allow. His signature with the date shows that he so orders the storekeeper. The use of a carbon sheet has entered the same information upon the duplicate copy.

At this time the secretary will enter on the supply and textbook record card for each article in the column "Apportioned" the quantity of the article that he has ordered to be delivered, the date of his order, and the number of the requisition asking for the article. At the same time he will enter the same data in the column "Available" and the quantity obtained by subtracting the quantity just apportioned from the quantity previously available to get the quantity available for other requisitioners after the article is apportioned. This is done for each article on the requisition.

The original copy of the requisition is then filed and the duplicate is sent to the storekeeper as an order to him to deliver the goods on or before the date given.

The storekeeper takes from the storeroom the goods ordered, on the store's tag deducts the quantity to be issued, entering also the date, and delivers the goods to the room on or before the date given in the requisition. He has the teacher check the items to show they have been delivered. She also signs her name to the form and writes the date to show that the goods checked have been received on the date given. The one delivering the goods also puts his signature on the sheet and the date of delivery. At this time the principal being notified of

106   School Costs and School Accounting

_____
_____ Janitor   _____ 191__   The work as described and
Work has been ordered done on Principal _____ 191__   fied has been done in a satisfact
_____   _____ 191__   _____
           Secretary   _____ 191__   Janitor
                                                      _____
                                                                Principal

_____
_____ Janitor   _____ 191_
Work has been ordered done on Principal _____ 191_
_____   _____ 19_
           Secretary   _____ 19_

Requisition Number

_____
_____ Janitor   _____ 191__   Work was completed on
Work has been ordered done on Principal _____ 191__
                                         _____ 191__

Work Requisition

the receipt of goods checks the delivery on his copy and enters the date.

The storekeeper or moveman, whoever delivers the goods, then forwards the receipt to the secretary who checks from the receipt the articles delivered, enters the date of delivery on the original copy and signs his name.

The secretary enters on the supply and text-book record card of each item received on requisition, in the column "Issued," the date on which the goods were delivered to the school room, the quantity, the number of the requisition, and subtracts the same quantity from the quantity "On Hand," entering in the latter column the date and the quantity on hand after the last issue. On the requisition the secretary will enter opposite "Issue Entered and Balanced" his initials and the date, showing that this operation has been performed.

The secretary will then enter on the grade ledger sheet for the grade the date of delivery of the goods, their description if so desired, the requisition number, and under "Instruction," "Supplies," their cost as shown on the requisition. Opposite "Issue Charged Against Proper *Division*" on the requisition the secretary will show that he has performed this operation by entering his initials and the date.

The same form of requisition may be used by the principal in requesting goods for his office or for the school as a whole. The operations to be performed will be the same, except that the secretary will enter the cost on the proper school ledger sheet under "Administration," "Supplies."

The requisition used by janitors is the same as that for teachers, except for the substitution of the word janitor for teacher, and the omission of the number of the grade. The procedure to be followed is the same as that for a principal's requisition; i.e., the charge is made against the proper school in the ledger under "Operation," "Janitorial Supplies," or other object.

Some standard form is also necessary to request that repair work or other miscellaneous services be performed. Such a requisition, which is made out in triplicate, is shown in the illustration. The original copy contains the following:

1. The designation of the place where the work is to be done —the number of the room.

2. The number of the grade when the work to be done is in any class room.

3. The name of the school.

4. The latest date on which the work should be done.

5. The description of the work.

6. The signature of the janitor with date of same.

7. The endorsement of the principal with date of same.

8. The signature of the secretary with date of same showing whether the work has been ordered done.

9. The initials of the secretary with date showing that the principal has been notified whether or not work has been ordered done.

10. The initials of the secretary with date showing that the work has been done.

11. The initials of the secretary with date showing that the voucher ordering payment has been acted upon favorably, giving also the number of the voucher.

12. The initials of the secretary with date, showing that the cost has been charged on the ledger sheet of the proper division, also giving the amount of cost.

On the duplicate and triplicate copies there are the same entries except for the last three items. For these on the duplicate there are substituted the following:

1. The signature of the janitor with date showing that the work has been done as described and specified in the requisition.

2. The signature of the principal with date endorsing the same statement.

On the triplicate copy, in place of the last three entries of the original, there is entered the date on which the work is completed.

The following procedure takes place in the use of this requisition:

When any work must be done in a school the janitor enters on the "Work Requisition Form" in duplicate the number of the room and the number of the grade, if it is a room in which instruction takes place that needs to have the work done. If it is the principal's office or a part of the heating plant not in any class room, such should be entered on the form. If the work is to be done on some part of the building or grounds used by

Description of Expenditure Documents Recommended 109

all pupils, the name of the school only should be entered. There is also given the latest date on which the work should be done. Also the janitor will give such description and specifications of the work to be done, in so far as such is possible, as will enable the secretary to make use of his description in checking the vendor's bill before certifying to its correctness. The janitor signs his name and enters the date on which requisition is made. He turns it over to the principal who, if he sees fit, endorses it, entering the date of same. The principal forwards both copies to the secretary, keeping the triplicate on file for reference.

The secretary examines the requisition, numbers it and the duplicate, decides himself or has the proper authorities decide as to whether the work should be done, arranges for its performance, orders it done and on both copies certifies to that effect by his signature, giving also the date on which the work is to be begun or done. The duplicate copy is then sent to the principal in order that he and the janitor may know that their request has been granted and that such preparations as are necessary may be made for the performance of the work. The secretary shows that he has notified the principal by entering his initials in the blank provided for the purpose giving the date of transmission of the order.

Upon completion of the work the janitor examines it to see that it meets the description and specifications in the requisition. Any variation in the work done from that requested is described in detail on the duplicate copy. The janitor then enters his name and the date certifying that the work done meets the specifications as he has revised them and is satisfactory. The principal makes a like certification, entering also the date. The duplicate copy is then returned to the secretary, who makes any changes necessary in the description in the original copy and enters his initials with the date showing that the work has been done. The bill rendered is compared with the report from the janitor. When the bill has been paid the voucher number is entered by the secretary together with his initials and the date. The cost is likewise entered in the proper blank and charged to the proper division in the ledger, the secretary showing by his initials and the date that such has been done. The original requisition is then filed.

_____ prepay transportation

Order Number _____
_____ 191__

Ship by _____

_____ prepay transportation

Order Number _____
_____ 191__

Ship by _____

_____ prep transportation

Order Number _____
_____ 191__

Ship by _____

Purchase Order

B. Purchase Orders

It is of course necessary for a board of education to make periodically many hundred purchases of various articles. The purchase order may be written throughout or the form may be standardized. Naturally the form has been standardized for most school systems. The form here used is made out in triplicate, the original being sent to the vendor, the duplicate being kept by the secretary and the triplicate being sent to the storekeeper.

The original copy provides for the following entries:

1. The date on which the order is issued.
2. The serial number of the order entered by the secretary to aid in identifying it.
3. The name and address of the vendor.
4. A blank with no entry requests prepayment of transportation, with "Do Not" inserted requests that transportation charges be not prepaid.
5. The designation of the means of transportation as by freight or express.
6. The quantity of goods desired.
7. The description of the goods ordered.
8. The signature of the secretary as the person transmitting the order.

The same entries are made on the duplicate and triplicate forms by the use of carbon sheets. The duplicate provides also for the following entries:

9. The initials of the secretary with date showing that he has entered on the supply and text-book record cards the quantities ordered.
10. The initials of the secretary with date showing that he has checked the goods received as indicated by the storekeeper with the duplicate copy of the original order.
11. The initials of the secretary with date showing that he has made the proper entries on the supply and text-book record cards, adding the quantities received to the quantities in stock and checking the quantities ordered in the column so headed on the same cards.

12. The initials of the secretary with date showing that he has compared the statement of the storekeeper as to quantities in stock with the quantities in stock as given on the supply and text-book record cards.

13. The initials of the secretary with date showing that he has written the vendor and notified the storekeeper of adjustments to be made in the shipment received.

The triplicate copy provides for the following entries in addition to the entries on the original copy:

9. The check of the storekeeper to show that each article received is as ordered; if not, the respect in which it is unsatisfactory.

10. The check of the storekeeper to show that each article received is as described in the invoice accompanying the shipment; if not, the respect in which they are unlike.

11. The quantity in stock as per the supply tag of each article of which there is a shipment.

12. The signature of the storekeeper with date showing that all goods have been received in satisfactory condition and as per invoice.

13. The signature of the secretary with date showing that all goods have been received in satisfactory condition and as per invoice.

The original form is filled out by the secretary and is sent to the vendor together with the form on which the vendor is to render his bill (to be described later). The duplicate copy is filed temporarily in the office of the secretary. The triplicate copy is sent to the storekeeper to notify him of the goods to be delivered. At the same time the secretary, on the supply and text-book record card of each article ordered, will enter in the column headed "Ordered" the date of the order, the quantity, and the order number. On his file copy in the blank provided the secretary will show that he has made such entry by writing his initials and the date.

Upon the receipt of the goods by the storekeeper he will examine them to see that they are satisfactory, that they are as ordered and as listed on the invoice. In the proper column all goods that are satisfactory and as ordered will be checked. If any articles are not satisfactory or do not fulfil the order, the storekeeper states the respect in which they are lacking.

In the next column the storekeeper checks all articles that are in accordance with the statement on the invoice. Those respects in which the goods do not correspond with the invoice are likewise stated. The storekeeper then enters on his supplies tag for each article, the date and quantity received and the total on hand. He will enter, in the proper column, on the triplicate for each article the quantity on hand, not of course including those that are unsatisfactory. The storekeeper then signs the copy, enters the date and returns the triplicate to the secretary.

The secretary checks on the duplicate copy of the order all goods received that are satisfactory according to the storekeeper's certification, after which he enters his initials in the proper blank together with the date to show that he has done this. The secretary then enters on the supply and text-book record card for each article in the column "In Stock" the date, the order number and the quantity received and enters the sum of the last entry and the quantity previously on hand. The order number in the column headed "Ordered" on which the goods were received is checked to show the receipt of the same. The secretary, after obtaining for each article the quantity on hand, compares it with the quantity on hand as given by the storekeeper on the triplicate. He shows that this operation has been performed by entering on the duplicate his initials and the date in the blank headed "Goods in Stock Compared."

Any adjustments that must be made are attended to by the secretary through correspondence with the vendor. The storekeeper is notified that such is the case by the receipt a second time of the triplicate, the secretary showing that he has done this by entering his initials and the date in the proper space on the duplicate. The receipt of the goods in satisfactory condition and as invoiced is shown by the check made by the storekeeper as described above for the original receipt of the goods. Both the storekeeper and secretary perform for these articles the same operations as for the goods originally received. The duplicate copy is then filed to compare with the bill rendered by the vendor.

C. Purchase Order Vouchers

With the original purchase order there will be sent the form to be used by the vendor in rendering his bill. On its face this form contains the following entries:

1. The date on which the bill is rendered.
2. The name and address of the vendor to whom the board of education is debtor.
3. The number of the order on which goods were delivered.
4. The quantity of goods sold.
5. The description of the goods.
6. The price of the goods per unit.
7. The amount of the cost for each item.
8. The total amount due on the bill.

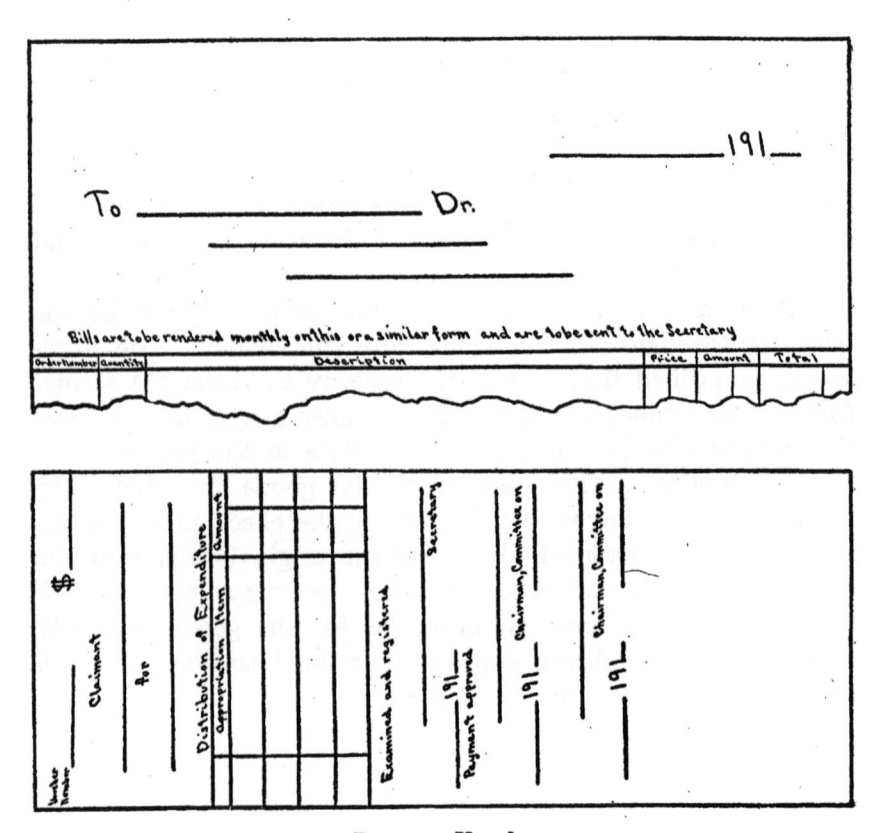

Payment Voucher

Description of Expenditure Documents Recommended 115

This bill when properly endorsed as shown on the reverse side, becomes a voucher for the propriety of paying the vendor for the services or things contained in it and is an order on the secretary to make such payment.

D. PAYROLLS, TIME SHEETS, AND PAYROLL VOUCHERS

The payroll on which are entered the salaries and wages of regular employees is made out for each school by the principal. The payrolls for elementary schools contain on their face the following entries:

1. The name of the school.
2. The month for which the payroll is made out.
3. The signature of the principal.
4. The date on which the payroll is made out.
5. The number of the grade which each teacher instructs.
6. The name of the teacher entered by the principal.
7. The number of days each person has taught during the month.
8. The monthly salary of each teacher.
9. The amount to be deducted for teachers' retirement fund, absence or other reason.
10. The difference between the last two entries or the amount due each person for services rendered.
11. The signature of the teacher showing that she has received the amount due.
12. The total for teaching.
13. Similar entries for the principal and
14. For the janitor or janitors of the school.
15. The total amount paid for personal service in the school.

On the reverse of the payroll is the voucher of the proper school authorities approving the bill for payment.

With the payroll there will be submitted by the principal a copy of his time sheet for the month containing the following information:

1. The name of the month and the year for which the statement is rendered.
2. The signature of the principal making the statement.
3. The date on which the statement is made.

116 School Costs and School Accounting

Payroll for Elementary Schools
_____School Month

_____   _____191__
         Principal

Elementary School Payroll

Elementary School Principal's Time Sheet

4. The name of the school for which the statement is made.
5. The amount of time spent each day in administration.
6. The amount of time spent each day in supervision.
7. The amount of time spent each day in supervision in each room.
8. The total amount of time spent in supervision of each room.
9. The amount of time spent in supervision of each grade.
10. The amount of the principal's salary to be charged to each grade.

The payrolls and time sheets to be used for high schools are the same as those for elementary schools, except that in place of the numbers of the grades being given there will be listed the subjects taught.

The payroll for supervisors and special teachers follows the same plan as that for high school teachers. It is, however, made out by the secretary instead of principal.

The time sheet shown in the illustration is to be used to get the data necessary to know the cost of supervision and special teaching for each division of the school system. The sheet provides for the following entries:

1. The month and year of which the following is a statement of service.
2. The name of the supervisor or special teacher whose the time sheet is.
3. The date on which it is completed.
4. For each day of school the name, abbreviated, of the school visited.
5. The number of each grade visited.
6. The number of minutes in hours and decimal parts of hours spent in each grade.
7. The total time spent in supervision, or special teaching each day.
8. The total time spent in supervision for the month.

On the reverse of the time sheet for the supervisors and special teachers is the summary by school and grade of the time spent in supervision or special teaching and the cost for the same. There is provision for the following entries:

1. The name of each school visited.
2. The time spent in supervision or special teaching in each grade in each school.

Supervisors' and Special Teachers' Payroll
Month of _____for_____ 191__

_____   ____191__
   Secretary

Reverse

1. *Supervisors' and Special Teachers' Payroll*
2. *Supervisors' and Special Teachers' Time Sheet—Face*
3. *Supervisors' and Special Teachers' Time Sheet—Reverse*

3. The cost for supervision or special teaching in each grade of each school.

4. The total cost for supervision or special teaching in each school.

5. The total cost of supervision or special teaching in each grade of all schools.

6. The total cost of supervision or special teaching by the person reporting on the time sheet.

A fourth payroll form is that used for employees of the school system other than those engaged in administration directly chargeable to particular schools, in supervision, instruction, and operation. This payroll provides for these entries:

1. The month and year for which it is rendered.
2. The signature of the secretary as the one making out the payroll.
3. The date on which it is made out.
4. The position of the person whose name appears on the roll.
5. The name of each payee.
6. The length of time for which he is to be paid.
7. The monthly rate of pay of each person.
8. The amount of deductions.
9. The amount due each person.
10. The signature of each payee.
11. The total amount due on the payroll.

On the reverse side of this payroll and each of those described, there is the same form of voucher as was previously described as on the reverse of bills rendered.

The procedure to be followed in the use of the payrolls is evident from the forms.

Each elementary school teacher's payroll is made out by the principal who enters for each teacher the number of the room and the number of the grade that she teaches, her name and the number of days she has taught during the month. The principal also enters his own name and that of the janitor or janitors with the periods of service.

At the same time the principal fills out his time sheet from his daily memoranda. He enters the month and year, the name of his school, his own name and the date on which the time sheet is made out. For each school day during the month he enters under "Administration" the time spent in performing that function, under "Supervision" the time spent in that service, and under the numbers denoting classrooms the amount of time spent in supervision in each room. The sum of all the last group of entries for each day should equal the entry for supervision. The total of each column is found and entered. From this is obtained the total for each grade. The principal forwards the payroll and his time sheet to the secretary who enters on the payroll the monthly salary of each teacher, the principal and janitors, the amount deducted, the amount due, and totals the amount due for teaching and the total amount due for the school. The time sheet is filed until the persons named are ordered paid.

The procedure to be followed with the high school payroll is the same as that for the elementary school payroll. The principal likewise makes out his time sheet, charging his time to the subjects taught in the classes he has supervised rather than to classrooms.

The payrolls for supervisors and special teachers and for sundry persons are made out in the office, the supervisors and special teachers having turned in their time sheets. The secretary then treats each payroll as a bill rendered, the procedure of which has already been described in the discussion of the form used by vendors in rendering bills for supplies.

When the payrolls are returned to the secretary with payment approved they are sent to the schools or offices to be signed by the persons named, showing their receipt of the amounts due them. When thus endorsed they are returned to the secretary to be filed with the other vouchers. Before doing this, however, the secretary enters in the ledger the cost of personal service during the period. The procedure will be as follows:

The secretary will charge in the ledger each grade for the amount paid for instruction, entering on the grade ledger sheet the date of the payroll, the description of the service if desired, the number of the voucher and the amount spent for personal service for instruction. The amount paid to janitors will be entered on the school ledger sheet in the same manner for personal service for operation. Before posting the amount paid to the principal it will be necessary to analyze the principal's time sheet. The costs of administration and supervision are determined on the basis of time spent in each. Likewise the cost of supervision for each grade is determined on the basis of the time spent in supervising each grade. That is,

Cost of administration = time spent in administration ÷ total time × amount paid for administration.

Cost of supervision = time spent in supervision ÷ total time × amount paid for supervision.

Cost of supervision in Room 8 = time spent in supervision in Room 8 ÷ total time spent in supervision × total cost of supervision.

The costs obtained are entered as indicated on the principal's time sheet. The cost of administration is then posted to the proper school ledger sheet where the entry is made for personal service for administration. The total for supervision is disregarded. The cost of supervision for each grade is posted to the proper grade ledger sheet where it is entered for personal service for supervision.

The same procedure is followed with the high school ledger, the charges being made, however, to the various subjects instead of rooms.

Again, the same general procedure is followed with the supervisors' and special teachers' payroll. In order to get the required costs for supervision it is necessary to go through the time sheets of all the supervisors in each subject and total for each school and each grade in each school the time spent in supervision in such school and grade. These will be totalled and the cost of supervision in each subject will be obtained on the basis of the time spent in supervision in each grade. That is, cost of supervision of drawing in Room 8 = time spent in supervision of drawing in Room 8 ÷ total time spent in supervision of drawing × total cost of supervision of drawing. These amounts are then posted to the proper grade ledger sheets for personal service for supervision. This is done for each subject. The same procedure is followed in the case of the special teachers' time sheets.

The payroll of sundry persons will be treated as the other payrolls. However, the charge will be to personal service for general administration.

CHAPTER XV

DESCRIPTION AND USE OF THE VARIOUS LEDGERS RECOMMENDED

A. Expense Ledger

The ledgers used are of four kinds, appropriation ledger, expense ledger, supply and text-book ledger, and permanent property ledger.

The following entries will be provided for on the grade ledger sheets of the expense ledger:

1. The number of the grade or the subject taught.
2. The name of the school.
3. The date on which services or things were furnished.
4. The description of services or things furnished.
5. The voucher number.
6. The requisition number.
7. The cost of personal service for instruction.
8. The cost of supplies for instruction.
9. The cost of various services for instruction.
10. The cost of personal service for supervision.
11. The cost of various services for supervision.
12. The cost of personal service for maintenance.
13. The cost of various services for maintenance.

The school ledger sheet contains provision for the following entries:

1. The name of the school.
2. The date when the account on the sheet is opened.
3. The date of any transaction occurring for the benefit of the school.
4. The description of the services or supplies furnished, if such is desired.
5. The voucher number.
6. The requisition number.
7. The cost of personal service for administration.
8. The cost of supplies for administration.

9. The cost of communication services.
10. The cost of various services for administration.
11. The cost of maintenance for administration.
12. The cost of personal service for operation.
13. The cost of janitorial supplies.
14. The cost of fuel.
15. The cost of light.
16. The cost of water.

General Administration Sheet

17. The cost of other supplies for operation.
18. The cost of various services for operation.
19. The cost of personal service for maintenance of the operating plant and equipment.
20. Other costs for the same.
21. The cost of personal service for maintenance of the school plant that is not for administering or operating purposes and that cannot be charged to any grade.
22. The cost of supplies for same.
23. Other costs for same.

The sheet is used by the secretary by entering all charges against a school, giving the date, description if desired, the voucher number or requisition number, and entering the cost in the proper column or columns.

Ledger sheets for other expenses will take the forms desired showing the characters and objects of expense so far as possible. Such a sheet is shown for general administration.

124   School Costs and School Accounting

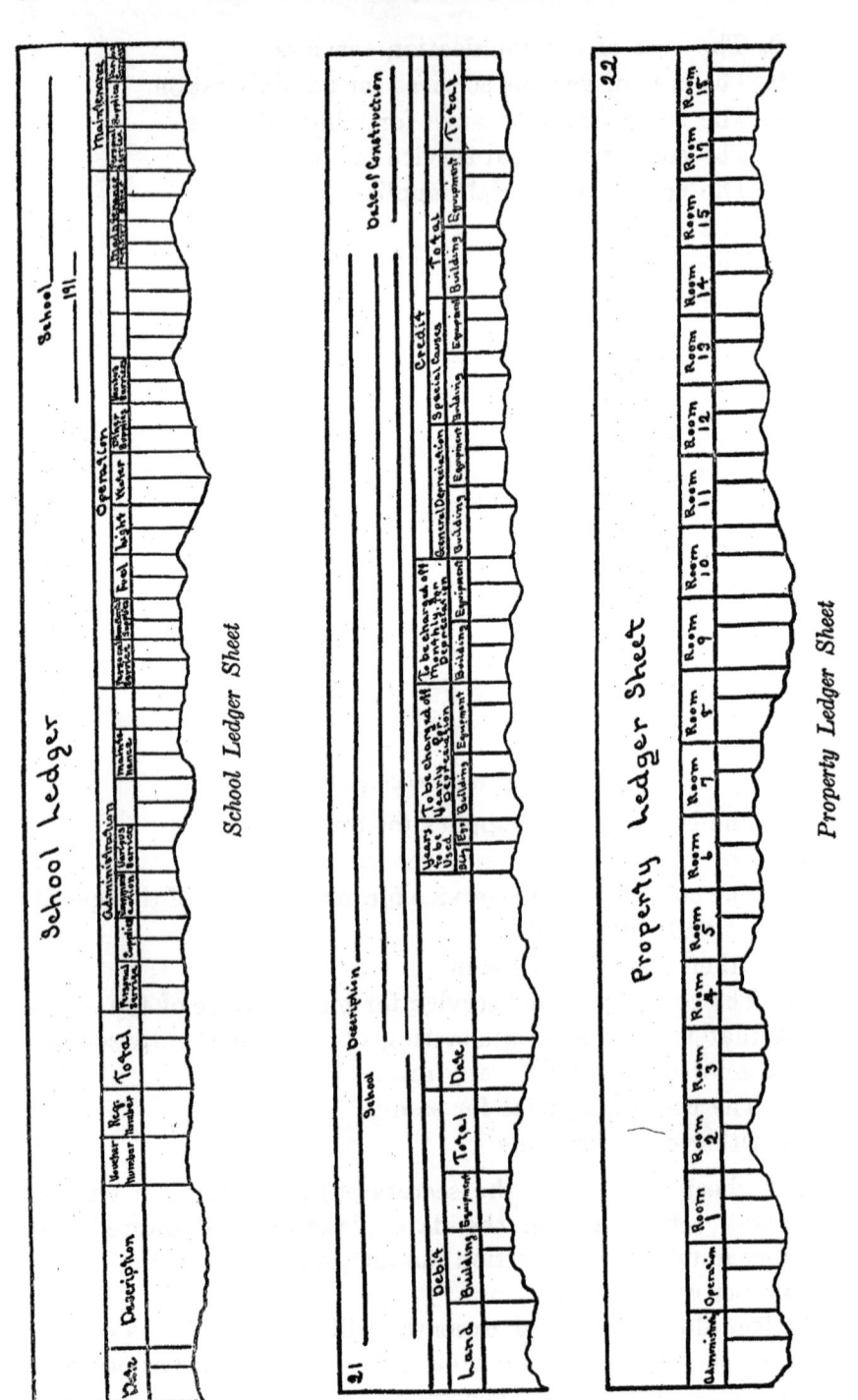

School Ledger Sheet

Property Ledger Sheet

B. Property Ledger

A third class of ledger accounts consists of those that show the value of the school property and the charges that are made against it. The property ledger sheet provides for the following entries:

1. The name of the school of which the sheet shows the record of property.
2. The date on which the account is opened on the sheet.
3. The date of the original construction of the building.
4. The description of the building, so far as such can be given on three lines.
5. The cost of land originally purchased for the school and of any additions.
6. The cost of the building as originally constructed and of all additions or other improvements to the building that increase its value.
7. The cost of the equipment originally placed in the building and of any new equipment that increases the value of the equipment already in the school.
8. The date of the transaction.
9. The description of the transaction.
10. The number of years the building or any addition to it is estimated to be in use.
11. The number of years it is estimated the equipment possessed and purchased is to be in use.
12. The amount that it is estimated that the value of the building or any addition to it will decrease each year; obtained by dividing the cost by the number of years it is estimated the building or addition will be in use.
13. The amount that it is estimated the value of the equipment will decrease each year; obtained as above described.
14. The amount that it is estimated the value of the building or any additions will decrease during each month of use; obtained by dividing the yearly decrease in value by the number of months in use.
15. Likewise, the amount that it is estimated the value of the equipment will decrease during each month of use.
16. The amount of depreciation, obtained as described above, that is credited to the value of the building or any addition.

17. The amount of depreciation, obtained as described above, that is credited to the value of the equipment.

18. The amount of decrease in value of the building due to other causes.

19. The amount of decrease in value of the equipment due to other causes.

20. The total amount of depreciation to be charged against the value of the building.

21. The total amount of depreciation to be charged against the value of the equipment.

22. A column each for administration, operation, and for each classroom in which is shown the division or divisions of the school in which the transactions take place.

When a school building has been constructed, the secretary learns the cost of the land, the cost of the building, the cost of the equipment and enters them as debits to the school. The cost of equipment for each division of the school building is then determined and is entered in the proper column as the detailed analysis of the investment for equipment. The secretary then determines the number of years it is estimated the building will be used. He calculates the amount of depreciation each year and the amount of depreciation each month on both building and equipment. At the end of each month he will credit to the building its depreciation for the month and to the equipment its depreciation for the same period. He will also credit to building and equipment any loss in value due to fire, accident, or other causes.

The secretary will debit to buildings any change or addition that increases their value. Thus, an addition of two rooms is debited to the building; while redecorating the interior is charged to running expense and does not appear in this ledger. Suppose it is found that the furniture purchased for Room 9 is unsatisfactory and furniture is purchased to replace it. From the sheet giving the divisions it is learned that the furniture in Room 9 cost $1500.00, that it was expected to last ten years, that $150.00 was credited against it each year, and that therefore it is not now carried as an asset. So the cost of the new furniture is debited to the school and is extended to the column under Room 9. Room 4 had new furniture five years ago that was expected to last ten years, that cost $1600.00, of which $160.00 was credited to the school each year. After five years it was carried as an asset of $800.00. The furniture was found unsatisfactory and had to be replaced by furniture costing $1200.00. This furniture took the place of furniture that had not served its period of usefulness. The latter on the books was still worth $800.00, but was replaced by the former worth $1200.00. The increase in the permanent value of the school is the difference, $400.00; the remainder is charged to maintenance.

C. Supply and Text-Book Ledger

The supply and text-book ledger sheet provides for the following entries:

1. The name of the article or book.
2. A short description of the article or the name of the author of the book.
3. The quantity to be ordered when the quantity available equals or falls below the minimum.
4. The smallest quantity allowed to be available; when the quantity available equals or falls below the minimum the maximum quantity must be ordered.
5. The cost per unit of the article or book.
6. The date on which an order for articles or books is issued.
7. The number of the purchase order.
8. The quantity of goods ordered.
9. The checking of orders received.
10. The date on which goods are delivered.
11. The number of the requisition on which goods are delivered.
12. The quantity of goods delivered from stock.
13. The date when quantity of goods stated is received in stock.
14. The quantity of goods received in stock.
15. The date on which goods are reserved.
16. The number of the requisition on which goods are reserved.
17. The quantity of goods reserved for delivery but not delivered.
18. The date on which the quantity stated was made available.
19. The quantity of goods available, i.e., not reserved or delivered.

When the secretary orders any supplies or books to be sent to the storeroom, he enters on the record the date of the order, the quantity ordered and the number of the order. When he receives word from the storekeeper that the goods have been received, on the record for each article ordered he checks the proper order and enters in the column "In Stock" the number received together with the date. He adds the quantity in stock to the quantity previously in stock to get the number in stock after receipt of the last shipment. He also enters in the column headed "Available" the date of receipt of the article and the quantity, adding the latter to the quantity previously available to get the quantity available after receipt of shipment. Upon receipt of a requisition, if it is to be granted the secretary enters the quantity,

Supply and Text-book Record Sheet

the date and the number of the requisition in the column "Reserved for Delivery" to show that the quantity has been assigned to some division. The same quantity is entered in the "Available" column together with the date and is subtracted in order that the goods may not be delivered to some other division in case they are not at once delivered to the first. When the goods are delivered to the division the quantity so issued is entered in the column "Delivered from Stock" together with the date of delivery and the number of the requisition. At the same time the quantity issued is entered in the column "In Stock" and is subtracted from the quantity previously in stock to get the quantity in stock at this date, which also is entered in this column.

This record is of greatest use because it is a perpetual inventory of goods in the storeroom. Also reference to it will show at a glance the quantity of goods available for use, the quantity of goods actually in stock in the storeroom and the quantity ordered. The record can be balanced at any time by adding the quantity on hand to the total of the quantities issued, which result should equal the total of the quantities ordered. Likewise the total of the quantities reserved added to the quantity available should equal the total of the quantities ordered. No leaks in goods can take place in the storeroom without being detected by the secretary because of the storekeeper's statement with each issue of the quantity on hand which is compared with the quantity on hand as shown in the ledger.

D. Supply and Text-book Tag

The storekeeper makes out for each article kept in stores a supply tag fastened near the articles in store. The tag provides for the following entries:

1. The name of the article.
2. The date on which the article is delivered.
3. The number of the requisition on which the article is delivered.
4. The quantity delivered.
5. The quantity in stock.

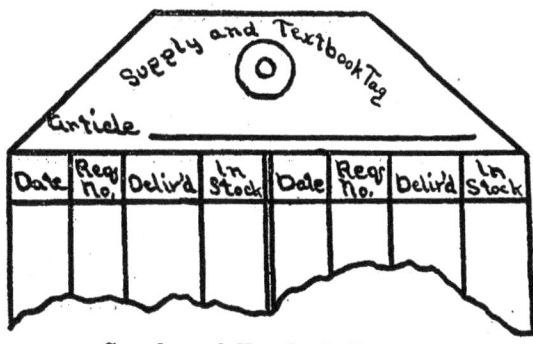

Supply and Text-book Tag

When the storekeeper receives from the secretary a requisition endorsed ordering him to deliver the goods as stated and takes the same from stores, for each article he enters on the tag the date of the delivery, the number of the requisition, the quantity delivered and the quantity in stock after deducting the quantity delivered. The storekeeper then enters on the requisition his initials and the date showing that he has made the entry, and gives the quantity of each article on hand after the delivery. By this means the secretary is able to check his records of deliveries and quantity in stock. When goods are received in the storeroom the storekeeper enters the date, the number of the order under requisition number, and the quantity in the column "In Stock" and enters the total in stock after the receipt of the goods.

Appropriation Ledger Sheet

E. APPROPRIATION LEDGER

The appropriation ledger sheets provide for the following entries:

1. The title of the appropriation.
2. The date on which the account on the sheet was opened.
3. The date of the transaction with the appropriation.
4. The description of the transaction in briefest form possible.
5. The numbers of the vouchers for credits to the appropriation.
6. The amount received on the appropriation.
7. The amounts credited to the appropriation.
8. The balance of the appropriation so arranged that it may be entered after each transaction.

The same form may be used for accounts receivable. From the ledger can be obtained at any time the amount on hand in any appropriation and the total balance of all appropriations.

CHAPTER XVI

DESCRIPTION AND USE OF FINANCIAL STATEMENTS

The worth of accounting is determined very largely by the use made of it to obtain data necessary to present periodically statements that picture clearly, accurately, comparatively, and in sufficient detail the present worth of the school plant, the expense incurred, the expenditures that have been made and the services that have been purchased. This is accomplished here by the use of four monthly statements, the general balance sheet, the statement of expenditures, the statement of expense, and the statement of unit costs.

A. GENERAL BALANCE SHEET

The balance sheet gives the total of all assets and of all liabilities, with the balance of assets over liabilities. The assets are classed as available and non-available, i.e., assets that are in such form that they may be used for the running expenses of the school system, and those that may not be used for such purpose. There are two classes of available assets, appropriations made by the municipality and accounts receivable, or money receivable from other sources such as the state, special taxes, and charges for tuition. Assets not available are property of the school system including land, buildings and equipment, funds set aside for more land, buildings and equipment, and supplies that are in the storeroom and in use in the schools.

The liabilities are classed as current, i.e., amounts owed by the school system for the running of the schools, and special, i.e., amounts owed by the school system for various special purposes. The current liabilities are taken from the audited vouchers showing the amount owed on each appropriation. Under special liabilities are listed all amounts owed that are not for the running expenses of the schools. These include the amounts of school bonds outstanding, interest and the like.

All of the above information is given not only for the present date but also for the month preceding and for the same date last year.

From this sheet it can be learned at a glance what the school system is worth at the date given, of what the assets of the system consist, how the assets of the school system vary with different periods. It should also make necessary questions concerning reasons for changes in the amounts of assets and liabilities for different periods.

The balances of the various appropriations are obtained from the appropriation ledger, where will also be entered the accounts

Not Available   Special
  Property + Other Fixed Assets
  Supplies in Store and in Use
  Funds for Capital Outlay   Total Liabilities
Total Assets   Balance

Monthly Balance Sheet

receivable. The amount of the property and fixed assets is obtained by totalling the balance of the accounts of the property ledger. The amount of funds for capital outlay is obtained from the appropriation ledger. The value of supplies in store is obtained by totalling the balances on the supply and text-book record cards. The value of the supplies in use is obtained by totalling the costs of all supplies and fifty per cent of the costs of all text-books reported as in use by the teachers' and principals' monthly returns. The amount of liabilities for special purposes will be learned by totalling the balances of such accounts in the appropriation ledger.

B. Statement of Expenditures

The purpose of the second statement is to show the conditions of the funds appropriated for school purposes. It is intended that there be printed in the column to the left the titles under which money is appropriated. The form provides for the following entries:

1. The month for which the statement is rendered.
2. The signature of the secretary who is responsible for the accuracy of the statement.
3. The title of each appropriation.
4. The date on which the secretary makes the statement.
5. The amount on hand in each appropriation on January first.
6. The amount received between January first and the present date.
7. The total amount received to the present date.
8. The amount expended up to the beginning of the present month.
9. The amount expended during the present month.
10. The total expended up to and including the last day of the month.
11. The difference between the amounts received up to and including the last day of the month and the amounts expended, i.e., the balance on hand.
12. The amounts that the school system is under contract to pay for services and things during the balance of the year.
13. The amounts that the school system will be obliged to pay during the rest of the year, not because it has contracted to do so, but because the charges are such as must be paid from year to year, such as interest, insurance, and rent.
14. The total amounts that the city must pay between the present date and the end of the year.
15. The difference between the amounts of funds on hand and the amounts that must be paid before the close of the year, i.e., the working balance of funds available for use as the authorities deem best.
16. All of the above information is given for the present year and for the same period of the preceding year.

Such a statement gives in detail all the information that is to be desired concerning funds entrusted to the board of education. It shows not only the sources of receipts, the amounts and the balances, but also the charges that will have to be met by the school authorities and the amounts available for general pur-

Monthly Statement of Expenditures

Monthly Property Statement

poses; a much more useful statement than simply that which shows receipts, expenditures, and balances. The statement also makes possible comparisons with the preceding year, great variations from which will always demand explanations.

All the information contained in the statement will be obtained from the appropriation ledger, except the charges fixed and contracted for during the remainder of the year.

C. Monthly Property Statement

The monthly property statement gives for each month the amount of the value of the property used for educational purposes. It provides for the following entries:

1. The name of the month for which it is a statement.
2. The signature of the secretary with date.
3. The name of the piece of property.
4. The value of the land.
5. The value of the buildings.
6. The value of the equipment.
7. The value of the books in its possession.
8. The value of the supplies in its possession.
9. The total value of all the assets of the piece of property under consideration.

This statement is made out monthly by the secretary who enters from the property ledger sheet of each school or other piece of property the present value of the land, buildings and equipment after the proper deductions have been made for depreciation and other charges. The present value of the books and supplies in the school is obtained from the monthly statement of supplies and text-books in the possession of the school as made out by the principal.

This statement of supplies and text-books in use is rendered to make it possible to know periodically the value of the assets of the school system that are in the schools and offices, not yet consumed, still of value to the city. The statement provides for the following entries:

1. The name of the school from which the report comes.
2. The name of the principal of the school.

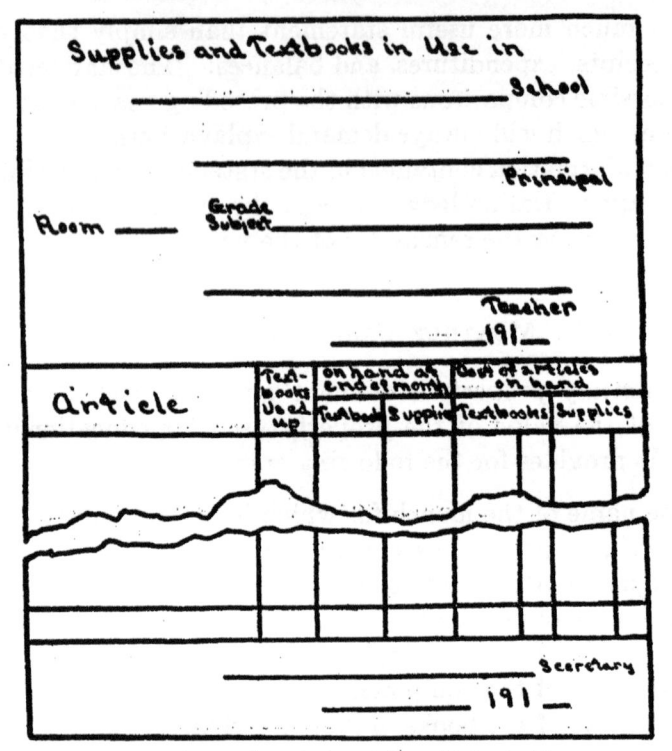

Statement of Supplies and Text-books in Use

3. The designation of the room for which report is made.

4. The name of the grade or subject if the report is made by a teacher.

5. The name of the person making the report.

6. The date on which the report is rendered.

7. The names of the articles reported.

8. The number of each title of text-books that are thrown aside during the month.

9. The number of each title of text-books on hand at the end of the month.

10. The quantity of each article of supplies on hand at the end of the month.

11. The cost of each number of text-books on hand.

12. The cost of each quantity of supplies on hand.

13. The initials of the secretary with date showing that he has determined the cost of text-books and supplies consumed and used during the month.

Just as far as possible the articles listed should be standardized so that the list may be printed as a part of the form. Three forms could be made, one for teachers' and pupils' text-books and supplies, another for principal's or administration supplies and a third for janitors' or operation supplies. The persons making the reports would then enter only the articles not listed together with the quantities asked for concerning all items. The report is made at the end of each month.

The person reporting enters the name of the school, the designation of the room, the name of the subject or the number of the grade where possible, his or her own name and the date of the report. For each article in the room or other division designated there is listed in the proper column the quantity on hand at the date of the report. The statement is turned over to the principal who by his signature shows his endorsement of it. The principal sends all the statements from the school to the secretary.

Upon receipt of the statements the secretary will enter upon each of them the cost of the quantity on hand of each text-book and article of supplies, and will total the same for the whole statement. He will compare the statements for each division as to text-books on hand with the records in the ledger to learn if the cost of books on hand plus the cost of those used up during the month equals the amount given in the ledger for the grade. The secretary will then enter on the monthly expense statement, as the cost of text-books for the grade, three per cent of the value of the books on hand at the beginning of the month as shown on the ledger sheets. In the total given on the monthly property statement he will enter as an asset fifty per cent of the cost of the books. The secretary will also subtract the cost of the supplies on hand at the end of the month from the sum of the costs of the supplies on hand at the beginning of the month and issued to the division during the month, and enter the difference on the monthly expense sheet as the cost of supplies for the division during the month. The cost of the supplies on hand at the end of the month is listed with the assets of the schools on the monthly property statement.

The rates three per cent and fifty per cent used in determining the cost and value of text-books are based upon the opinion that the usefulness of such articles continues between three and four years and that at any given time the average value of all text-books in use is one half the original value.

If text-books can be used for three years before being cast aside, their value decreases one third yearly; if they are used ten months in the year their value decreases each month one thirtieth. The percentage here used allows an additional third of a year for books to last, making the rate of monthly decrease in value three per cent of the original cost. The choice of rate is of course arbitrary. Yet by its use there is charged to each division using the school system a certain loss in value of text-books, one of the system's assets, that is as just a rate as can be used unless the per cent of loss is determined scientifically as it has not yet been, but should be.

Likewise the use of fifty per cent of the original cost as the amount of the present value of text-books in use is the result of an arbitrary decision that the value of books varies normally from zero in the case of books just thrown aside to one hundred per cent of the original cost as the value of books just purchased. Neither supposition is correct because books thrown aside are still of some small value and books just purchased cannot be sold for the original price. However, the use of the rate does make possible the inclusion of text-books as an asset of the school system and is as just as any rate that can be used unless the monthly and yearly rate of loss of value is determined scientifically.

D. Distribution of Expense Sheet

But for purposes of efficiency in education and school administration the two following statements are most useful. By these the school administrator is able to learn facts concerning the work of his school that he could get in no other way. From their study he is able to learn where the leaks are in the work of his school and to repair them so that he gets the maximum of service out of his resources. By the statements a superintendent is able to learn not only what janitor is wasting fuel, what teacher is wasting supplies, but what principal is wasting his service, what supervisor is wasting her service. The superintendent can detect what grade is receiving more or less than its share of instruction and of supervision by principal and by supervisor. The statements are two in number, the first a statement of expense for each school and grade, the second a statement of expense for each pupil in average daily attendance in each school and grade. To be worth while the statements must be complete and accurate, i.e., to each school must be charged all the expenses incurred within it and because of it. Likewise for each grade there must be charged to it all expenses incurred within and because of it. This means that there must be charged to each division of the school system all the expense incurred that is chargeable directly to it and in addition a proportion of all indirect expense that is as nearly accurate as it is possible to be. In order that these ends may be obtained there is explained here a method by which all the charges direct and indirect may be made to the proper divisions so that a true measurement of costs is obtained.

On Sheet 1 for general administration and on sheets for each school similar to Sheet 2 there are entered all the direct charges that may be obtained from the expense ledger. Thus for general administration items 1 and 5 will be entered from the general administration ledger sheet. Items 1 through 5, and 7 through 21 for each school will be obtained from the school ledger sheets. Likewise items 33 through 42 for the grades will be obtained from the grade ledger sheets. In all cases the cost of supplies is obtained by subtracting from the sum of the costs of the supplies on hand at the beginning of the month plus the cost of supplies received during the month, the cost of the supplies on hand at the end of the month, plus three per cent of the value of the text-books on hand in the division at the beginning of the month.

These steps and the following steps are all explained on the expense distribution sheet. After all the direct expenses have been entered and totalled there must be made a proper distribution of indirect expense.

No exact method of charging to each division of a building its exact share of operating expense is known. $1,000.00 may be spent for fuel but just how much of that was used in heating Room 8 last month and this month is not known. Exactly how much it costs to clean Room 8 each day cannot be known because there is no time clock at the entrance to the room where the janitor can register the time of his beginning and ending work, nor is there any one to issue to him the necessary supplies when he enters and take what is left when he comes out, to get the

140   School Costs and School Accounting

EXPENSE DISTRIBUTION FOR MONTH OF _____

Sheet 1

_____ 191___
Secretary

_____ 191___

Order of Procedure	Directions for Distribution of Expense	Character and Object of Expense	Order of Procedure			General Administration
		Personal Service	1			
		Supplies	2			
		Communication	3			
		Various Services	4			
		Maintenance	5			
		Total Direct Expense	6			
		Indirect Expense	26			
		Total General Administration	27			
		Operation and Maintenance Rate	25			
				28	29	
		Name of School		Average Daily Attendance	General Administration Expense Rate	
1 to 5 incl.	Enter in the proper columns the amounts asked for opposite the numbers 1 to 5 inclusive					
6	Enter at 6 the total direct administration expense obtained by adding amounts 1 through 5					
7 to 15 incl.	Enter in the proper columns the amounts asked for opposite the numbers 7 through 15					
16	Enter at 16 the total operation expense obtained by adding amounts 7 through 15					
17 to 19 incl.	Enter in the proper columns the amounts asked for opposite the numbers 17 through 19					
20	Enter at 20 the total maintenance expense obtained by adding the amounts 17 through 19					
21	Enter at 21 the amount of depreciation					
22	Enter at 22 the total direct expense obtained by adding amounts 6; 16; 20; 21					
23	Enter at 23 the total expense for operation maintenance and depreciation obtained by adding 16; 20; 21					
24	Enter at 49 through 54 the data asked for. Determine for the general administration office, each school administration office and for each grade its operation and maintenance number and enter each at 24					
25	Calculate and enter at 25 the operation and maintenance rate for the general administration office and for each school administration office; i. e., divide the o. and m. number of each by the total o. and m. number					
26	Distribute to general and school administration their shares of operation and maintenance expense; i. e., multiply the amount at 23 by the rates entered at 25					
27	Enter at 27 the total of general expense obtained by adding amounts 6 and 26					
28	Enter at 28 the average attendance of each school and all schools					
29	Calculate and enter at 29 the general administration expense rate for each school; i. e., divide the average daily attendance of each school by the total average daily attendance of all schools					
30	Distribute the general administration expense rate to each school; i. e., multiply the total for general administration at 27 by the general administration expense rate for each school and enter the amounts at 30					
31	Enter at 31 the amount of operation and maintenance expense to be distributed to the grades; i. e., subtract amount 26 from amount 23					
32	Enter at 32 the amount of total expense obtained by adding the amounts 22 and 30					
33 to 35 incl.	Enter in the proper columns the amounts asked for opposite the numbers 33 through 35					
36	Enter at 36 the total spent for supervision					
37 to 39 incl.	Enter in the proper columns the amounts asked for opposite the numbers 37 through 39					
40	Enter at 40 the total spent for instruction					
41	Enter at 41 the total spent for maintenance					
42	Enter at 42 the total direct expense obtained by adding the amounts 36; 40; 41					
43	Enter at 43 the average daily attendance of each grade and all grades					
44	Calculate and enter the school administration expense rate for each grade; i. e., for each school divide the average attendance of each grade by the total average attendance for the school					
45	Distribute the administration expense to each grade; i. e., for each school multiply the total expense for administration by the administration rate for each grade and enter the amount at 45					
46	Calculate the operation and maintenance expense rate for each grade; i. e., divide the o. and m. number for each grade by the total of o. and m. numbers and enter the results at 46					
47	Distribute the operation and maintenance to each grade; i. e., multiply the total expense for o. and m. by the o. and m. rate for each grade and enter the amount at 47					
48	Enter at 48 the total expense obtained by adding the amounts 42; 45; 47					
		Total				

Expense Distribution Sheet—1

Description of Financial Statements

Expense Distribution Sheet—2

difference and to add to it the decrease in value of the brushes and brooms used in cleaning. The distribution must be more or less arbitrary; it should be the least arbitrary possible. The cost of cleaning a building or a room varies more or less closely with the area. The cost of heating a building varies more or less closely with the volume. The part of the cost of these two items to be borne by any part of a building should vary according to the time it is used. These three factors are used in determining the amounts to be distributed to each grade for the cost of operation and maintenance of a school building in so far as the maintenance cannot be charged directly to any room. The form shown on the back of each sheet is used. On it all the rooms used by Grade I are listed in the proper column. For each room there are entered its volume and its area and the product of these two numbers. All the products of rooms used by Grade I are totalled in the same column, the number of hours per week the rooms are in use is entered and the product of the last two numbers is entered as the number desired. If the room is used for manual training or for evening school instruction or for other purposes requiring the consumption of relatively more of any service or thing than other rooms, the number of hours in use should be doubled when used to compute the operation and maintenance number. The same is done for each grade, for each subject in the high school, for evening schools, for kindergartens and for administration. The operation and maintenance rate is obtained as stated in the procedure.

The cost of administration is distributed on the basis of average daily attendance because the cost of administration is to a great extent dependent upon the number of pupils in daily attendance. In determining the costs of evening school a two-hour session is considered as two-fifths of a school day. By the use of the expense distribution sheet there is charged to general administration its share of operating and maintenance expense, especially if the superintendent's office is in a school building. The expense for general administration is then distributed to each school and is merged with the cost of school administration which has itself received its share of the cost of operation and maintenance. Administration and operation and maintenance are then distributed to the various grades, so that finally there is known accurately what it has cost to do for one month for each grade that for which the schools exist.

E. Statement of Unit Costs

In the unit cost statement each of the amounts of expense has been divided by the proper number of pupils in average daily attendance in order to compare them with the previous average cost per pupil for the present year to date and for the previous year to the same date. The same comparisons are made of all the schools in the system.

The second part of this table compares the cost per pupil in each grade for each character of service, direct expense and indirect expense, with like costs of previous periods and with the same grades of other schools. Costs in the high school will be measured by dividing the cost of each subject by the average daily attendance multiplied by the number of recitations in the subject held during the month.

Monthly Statement of Unit Costs—Sheet 1

Description of Financial Statements

Costs Per Pupil in Average Daily Attendance for _____ in Each Grade

Sheet 2
191_
sec _____ 191_

Character of Expense	School 1			School 2			School 3			School 4		
	This Month	Average This year to Date	Average last year to Date	This Month	Average This year to Date	Average last year to Date	This Month	Average This year to Date	Average last year to Date	This Month	Average This year to Date	Average last year to Date
Grade I Supervision by Principal												
Supervision by Supervisors												
Instruction												
Maintenance												
Total Direct Expense												
Grade II Supervision by Principal												
Supervision by Supervisors												
Instruction												
Maintenance												
Total Direct Expense												
Grade III Supervision by Principal												
Supervision by Supervisors												
Instruction												
Maintenance												
Total Direct Expense												
Grade IV Supervision by Principal												
Supervision by Supervisors												
Instruction												
Maintenance												
Total Direct Expense												
Grade V Supervision by Principal												
Supervision by Supervisors												
Instruction												
Maintenance												
Total Direct Expense												
Grade VI Supervision by Principal												
Supervision by Supervisors												
Instruction												
Maintenance												
Total Direct Expense												
Grade VII Supervision by Principal												
Supervision by Supervisors												
Instruction												
Maintenance												
Total Direct Expense												
Grade VIII Supervision by Principal												
Supervision by Supervisors												
Instruction												
Maintenance												
Total Direct Expense												

Monthly Statement of Unit Costs—Sheet 2

CHAPTER XVII

CONCLUSION

Such a system of accounting as that recommended makes possible:

1. Original records for all financial transactions within the school system.

2. The accurate accounting for all school property and other assets of the city's schools.

3. The accurate accounting for all funds appropriated for school purposes.

4. The accurate determination of costs for all forms of education, for each kind of school, for each character of expense, and for each object of expense.

5. True comparisons of costs within the school system for the same period and with previous similar periods.

6. The detection of efficiency and inefficiency of service rendered.

7. When a sufficient number of cities make use of the system, the determination of standard unit costs for education, such as this investigation set out to determine.

That is, such a system of accounting will record continually, completely, and accurately all the data necessary both to show with fullness and exactness and at all times the condition of the city's school finances and also to prove the faithfulness or unfaithfulness and the efficiency or inefficiency of public officials entrusted by the municipality with property, funds, and powers for the education of its children.

INDEX

A, population of; financial statement of City, 16; total expenditures per pupil on all schools, Table XIV, 32; expenditures for each kind of school in City, 42.

Accounting, purposes of school, Ch. II, 4; purposes of, 6; first purpose of school, fidelity of school officials, 6; second purpose of school, determination of costs for aid in deciding policies, 8; third purpose of school, determination of unit costs to measure efficiency, 8; first defect, receipt and expenditure, only, not revenue and expense, 34; second defect, expenditures for maintenance and capital outlay not distinguished, 36; third defect, no, for expenditures by kind of school, 46; fourth defect, no, for expenditures by character of service, 52; fifth defect, no common classification of objects of expenditure, 55; information to be recorded for purposes of, 57; system recommended, purposes of, 98; results to be accomplished by system recommended, 145.

Accounts payable, copy of register of, in use in Newton, 78; copy of controlling record of, in use in Lynn, 79.

Administration, explanation of term, 47; a sub-function of education, 56; general, ledger sheet, 123; monthly statement of unit costs for general, and for each school, 144; distribution of expense of, 142.

All schools, cost per pupil on, Ch. VI, 32; expenditure per pupil on all schools, Table XIV, 32.

Amounts, increasing, spent by cities for education, 5; spent per pupil in average daily attendance, Ch. V, 20; spent per pupil for each object of school expenditure, Table XIII, 22; spent for operation in six cities, Table XIX, 51; spent per pupil for operation in six cities, Table XX, 51; spent per pupil for personal service in eight cities, Table XXI, 54.

Amsterdam, N. Y., population, 2.

Appropriation ledger sheet, recommended, 130; balance sheet recommended, 132.

Area, basis for expense distribution, 142.

Assets, classes of, 131.

Attendance, Cf. Average daily attendance.

Auburn, N. Y., population, 2; financial statement, 86.

Average daily attendance, amounts spent per pupil in, Ch. V, 20; on schools of twenty cities, Table XII, 20; reason for use of unit, 21; amounts spent per pupil in, for each object of school expenditure, Table XIII, 22; cost per pupil in, on all schools, Ch. VI, 32; expenditures per pupil in, on all schools, Table XIV, 32; cost per pupil in, on each kind of school, Ch. VII, 37; cost per pupil in, for each character of service, 47; expenditures per pupil in, for operation in six cities, Table XX, 51; cost per pupil in, for personal service, supplies, and various services, 53; expenditure per pupil in, for personal service in eight cities, Table XXI, 54; basis in computing unit costs, 143.

B, cost per pupil in City, 32.

Balance sheet, general, recommended, 131; appropriation, 132.

Bayonne, N. J., population, 2.

Beverly, Mass., population, 2; financial statements, 86.

Binghamton, N. Y., population, 2.

Bloomfield, N. J., population, 2.

Boards of Education, financial statements of some, Ch. IV, 12.

Book, record card, Montclair, 82. text-book record card, Malden, 84; requisition for books and supplies, recommended, 102; supply and text-book ledger recommended, 127; statement of supplies and text-books in use, recommended, 136.

148 Index

Brookline, Mass., population, 2.

C, financial statement of City, 15; expenditures per pupil on all schools in City, 32; expenditures for each kind of school in City, 37.

Capital outlay, distinction between maintenance and, 35; expenditure for maintenance and, not distinct, second defect, 36; explanation of term, 48; accounting for, 125.

Character of service, cost per pupil for each, Ch. VIII, 47; explanation of, 47; no accounting for expenditures by, fourth defect, 52.

Chelsea, Mass., population, 2.

Cities, number of, visited, 1; visited and their populations, 2; increasing amounts spent by, for education, 5; expenditures for education in certain, 12.

Classification, no common, of objects of expenditure, 55.

Cost, per pupil on all schools, Ch. VI, 32; per pupil on each kind of school, Ch. VII, 37; per pupil for each character of service, Ch. VIII, 47; per pupil for personal service, supplies, and various services, 53.

Costs, determination of standard unit, for education, purpose of investigation, Ch. I, 1; standard unit, their importance in education, 5; determination of, for aid in deciding policies, second purpose of school accounting, 8; determination of unit, to measure efficiency, third purpose of school accounting, 8; school, importance in education, 10; standard unit, for public education, 10; items for which unit, were sought, 11; information concerning expenditures only, none concerning, 33; statement of unit, recommended, 143.

D, cost per pupil in City, 32.

Daily attendance, Cf. Average daily attendance.

Data, method of collection of, 1; summary of, contained on requisitions, Table XXII, 58; on purchase orders, Table XXIII, 65; on payrolls, Table XXIV, 70; on vouchers, Table XXV, 75.

Defects in school accounting, first, receipt and expenditure accounting only, not revenue and expense, 34; second, expenditures for maintenance and capital outlay not distinguished, 36; third, no accounting for expenditures by kind of school, 46; fourth, no accounting for expenditures by character of service, 46; fifth, no common classification of object of expenditure, 55.

Definition of terms, standard unit costs for public education, 10; administration, 47; supervision, 48; instruction, 48; maintenance, 48; capital outlay, 48.

Depreciation, of buildings and equipment, 126; of text-books, 137.

Distribution, of expense sheet, 138; of operation expense, 139; of maintenance expense, 139; of administration expense, 142.

Documents of expenditure, description and use of, Ch. X, 56; recommended, 101.

E, financial statement of City, 17; expenditures per pupil on all schools in City, 32; expenditures for each kind of school in City, 44.

East Orange, N. J., population, 2.

Efficiency, in education, 4; determination of unit costs to measure, third purpose of education, 8.

Elementary schools, pay-roll and time-sheet for, recommended, 115; Cf. Kind of school.

Elmira, N. Y., population, 2.

Everett, Mass., population, 2; requisition for repairs, 64.

Expenditures, for education in certain cities, 12; per pupil, Ch. V, 20; per pupil for each object of school expenditure, Table XIII, 22; total, per pupil in average daily attendance on all schools, Table XIV, 32; information concerning, only, none concerning costs, 33; first defect, receipt and expenditure accounting only, not revenue and expense, 34; second defect, for maintenance and capital outlay not distinguished, 36; third defect, no accounting for, by kind of school, 46; for each kind of school in City C, Table XV, 37; City N, 39; City R, 39; City T, 41; City W, 42; City A, 42; City G, 44; City E, 44; City K, 44; City H, 46; cost per pupil for each character of expenditure, 47; for operation in six cities, Table XIX, 51; per pupil for operation in six cities, Table XX, 51; fourth defect, no accounting for, by character of service, 52; fifth defect, no common classification of objects of, 55; documents of, Ch. X, 56; documents of, recommended, 101; monthly statement of, recommended, 132.

Expense, receipt and expenditure accounting only none for revenue and, first defect, 34; ledgers recommended, 122; distribution sheet recommended, 138.

F, financial statement of City, 12; expenditures per pupil on all schools in City, 32;

Financial statement, of City X, 7; of same boards of education, Ch. IV, 12; of City F, 12; City L, 13; City M, 13; City V, 14; City T, 14; City C, 15; City A, 16; City E, 17; City W, 18; description and use of, Ch. XII, 86; in use in Auburn, 86; Beverly, 86; Little Falls, 89; Malden, 90; Lynn, 91; Newton, 92; Poughkeepsie, 96.

Financial statements recommended, description and use of, Ch. XVI, 131; general balance sheet, 131; of expenditures, 132; of property, 134; of supplies and text-books in use, 136; of unit costs for general administration and for each school, 144; of unit costs for each grade, 145.

Forms recommended, 99.

Framingham, Mass., population, 2.

Funds, *Cf.* Appropriations.

G, cost per pupil in City, 32; expenditure for each kind of school in City, 44.

General administration ledger sheet, recommended, 123, balance sheet 131.

Geneva, N. Y., population, 2.

Grade ledger sheet, recommended, 122.

H, cost per pupil in City, 32; expenditure for each kind of school in City, 46.

High school, pay-roll and time sheet for, recommended, 117. *Cf.* Kind of school.

Hoboken, N. J., population, 2.

Instruction, explanation of term, 48.

Investigation, purpose of the, determination of standard unit costs for education, Ch. I, 1; purpose of, explanation of, 10.

J, cost per pupil in City, 32.

K, cost per pupil in City, 32; expenditure for each kind of school in City, 44.

Kind of school, no accounting for expenditures by, third defect, 46; cost per pupil on each, Ch. VII, 37; expenditure for each, in City, C, 37; City N, 37; City R, 39; City T, 41; City W, 42; City A, 42; City G, 44; City E, 44; City K, 44; City H, 46.

L, financial statement of City, 13; expenditures per pupil on all schools in City, 32.

Lynn, Mass., population, 2; requisition, 62; purchase order, 67; controlling record of accounts payable, 79; school ledger, 80; stock book, 82; financial statement, 91.

Ledgers, description and use of various, Ch. XI, 77; register of accounts payable, Newton, 78; record of accounts payable, Lynn, 79; school ledger, Lynn, 80; Niagara Falls, 81; supply, in use, 81; stock book, Lynn, 82; book record card, Montclair, 82; stock room card, Schenectady, 83; book record card, Malden, 84; description and use of various, recommended, Ch. XV, 122; expense, 122; grade, 122; general administration, 1 2 3 ; school, 123; property, 125; supply and text-book 127; supply and text-book tag, 129; appropriation, 130.

Liabilities, classes of, 131.

Little Falls, N. Y., population, 2; financial statement, 89.

Lockport, N. Y., population, 2.

M, financial statement of City, 13; expenditures per pupil on all schools in City, 32.

150   *Index*

Maintenance, distinction between, and capital outlay, 35; expenditures for, and capital outlay not distinct, second defect, 36; explanation of term, 48; distribution of expense for, 139.
Malden, Mass., population, 2; requisition, 63; text-book record card, 84; financial statement, 90.
Marlborough, Mass., population, 2.
Melrose, Mass., population, 2.
Method, of collection of data, 1.
Montclair, N. J., population, 2; copy of book record, 82.
Mt. Vernon, N. Y., population, 2.

N, cost per pupil in City, 32; expenditure for each kind of school in City, 39.
New Brunswick, N. J., population, 2.
Newburgh, N. Y., population, 2.
New Rochelle, N. Y., population, 2.
Newton, Mass., population, 2; purchase order, 68; register of accounts payable, 78; financial statement, 92.
Niagara Falls, N. Y., population, 2; requisition, 62; ledger, 81.
Northampton, Mass., population, 2.

Object, amount spent per pupil for each, of school expenditure, Table XIII, 22; fifth defect, no common classification of objects of expenditure, 55; cost per pupil for personal service, supplies, and various services, 53.
Officials, fidelity of, first purpose of school accounting, 6.
Operation, explanation of term, 48; amounts spent for, in six Cities, Table XIX, 51; expenditure per pupil for, in six cities, Table XX, 51; distributing expense for, 139.
Orange, N. J., population, 2.
Orders, *Cf.* Purchase order.
Outlay, *Cf.* Capital outlay.

P, cost per pupil in City, 32.
Passaic, N. J., population, 2.
Payrolls, in use, 68; Poughkeepsie, 69; voucher recommended, 115; recommended for elementary schools, 115; for high schools, 117; for supervisors and special teachers, 117; for sundry persons, 119.
Personal service, cost per pupil for, supplies, and various services, 53; expenditure per pupil for, in eight cities, 54.

Populations, cities visited and their, 2.
Port Chester, N. Y., population, 2.
Poughkeepsie, N. Y., population, 2; copy of pay-roll, 69; financial statement, 96.
Property ledger sheet, recommended, 125; monthly property statement recommended, 135.
Purchase orders, in use, 64; summary of data contained on, 65; Lynn 67; Newton, 68; recommended, 110; voucher recommended, 114.
Purpose, of the investigation, determination of standard unit costs for education, Ch. I, 1; of school accounting, Ch. II, 4; three, of school accounting, 6; of the investigation, explanation of, 10; information to be recorded for, of accounting, 57; of accounting system recommended, Ch. XIII, 98.

R, cost per pupil in City, 32; expenditure for each kind of school in City, 39.
Receipt, and expenditure accounting only, none for revenue and expense, first defect, 34.
Recommended, accounting system, 98.
Register, of accounts payable, Newton, 78; controlling record of accounts payable; Lynn, 79.
Repairs, *Cf.* Maintenance.
Requisitions, in use, 57; Niagara Falls, 62; Lynn, 62; Malden, 63; for repairs, Everett, 64; recommended, 101; recommended for text-books and supplies, 102; recommended for work, 106.
Revenue and expense, receipt and expenditure accounting only, none for, first defect, 34.
Revere, Mass., population, 2.

S, cost per pupil in City, 32.
Schenectady, N. Y., population, 2; stock room record card, 83.
School accounting, *Cf.* Accounting.
School costs, *Cf.* Costs.
Service, cost per pupil for each character of, Ch. VIII, 47; explanation of character of, 47; no accounting for expenditures by character of, fourth defect, 52.
School ledger sheet, recommended, 123. g
Somerville, Mass., population, 2.
Stamford, Conn., population, 2.

Standard, *Cf.* Unit costs.
Standardization, in education, 4.
Statement, *Cf.* Financial statements.
Stock, book, Lynn, 82; room record card, Schenectady, 83.
Summary, of data contained on requisitions, 58; on purchase orders, 65; on pay-rolls, 70; on vouchers, 75.
Sundry persons, pay-roll and time sheet for, 119.
Supervision, explanation of term, 47.
Supervisors and special teachers, pay-roll and time sheet for, recommended, 117. *Cf.* Character of service. *Cf.* Supervision.
Supplies, cost per pupil for personal service, and, and various services, 53; requisition for text-books and, recommended, 102; statement of, and text-books in use, recommended, 136.
Supply, ledgers in use, 81; and text-book ledger recommended, 127; and text-book tag recommended, 129.

T, financial statement of City, 14; expenditures per pupil on all schools in City, 32; expenditures for each kind of school in City, 41.
Tag, supply and text-book recommended, 129.
Teachers, *Cf.* Character of service. *Cf.* Instruction.
Text-books, *Cf.* Book.
Time sheet, pay-roll and, for elementary schools, recommended, 115; for high schools, 117; supervisors' and special teachers, 117; sundry persons; 119.
Time used, basis for expense distribution, 142.

U, cost per pupil in City, 32.
Unit, reason for use of average daily attendance, 21; of volume, time used, area, as bases for distributing expense, 142.
Unit costs, determination of standard, for education, purpose of investigation, Ch. I, 1; standard, their importance in education, 5; determination of, to increase efficiency, third purpose of school accounting, 8; standard for public education, definition of terms, 10; items for which, were sought, 11; statement of, recommended, 143.
Utica, N. Y., population, 2.

V, financial statement of City, 14; expenditures per pupil on all schools in City, 32.
Various services, cost per pupil for personal service, supplies, and, 53.
Volume, basis for expense distribution, 142.
Vouchers, in use, 73; Yonkers, 74; summary of data contained on, 75; purchase order, recommended, 114; pay-roll, recommended, 115.

W, financial statement of City, 18; expenditures per pupil on all schools in City, 32; expenditures for each kind of school in City, 42.
Work requisition, recommended, 106.

X, financial statement of, 7.

Yonkers, N. Y., population, 2; voucher in use in, 74.

VITA

J. HOWARD HUTCHINSON, born at Hamilton, N. Y., February 7, 1883.

Graduate, Colgate Academy, 1901; Colgate University, A.B., 1905; Columbia University, A.M., 1909.

Principal of schools in New York State, 1905–08; 1909–12.

Graduate student in educational administration, Teachers College, 1908–12.

Member of Training School for Public Service, Bureau of Municipal Research,—investigation of scientific management as applicable to municipal operations, surveys of schools and of other departments of city government, and investigation of various municipal government problems, 1912.